The Advantage

How to Successfully Navigate Life with the Holy Spirit as Your Competitive Edge and Best Friend

By

Dr. Corletta J. Vaughn

Copyright © 2021 by Dr. Corletta J. Vaughn All Rights Reserved

All rights reserved, including the rights to reproduce this book or portions thereof in any form or by any means whatsoever including electronic, mechanical, photocopying, recording, or by any information storage and retrieval system without written permission of the publisher, except for the including of brief quotations in a review.

First Ebook/Paperback Edition:

January 2021

For information about:

"Living With The Advantage"

Contact Author:

Dr. Corletta J. Vaughn

Website: www.gotellit.org

Email: corlettavaughn@gmail.com

Created in the United States of America

DEDICATION PAGE

To Shannon Marie and Apprille Nicole, my two children, who have been with me on this amazing adventure their entire lives.

To Ruth Sinclair, my sister, who has watched it all play out up-close and personal.

To all who have encountered Holy Spirit through something I have said, written, or lived.

and...

To all the people on their way to Pentecost.

ACKNOWLEDGMENT

Thank you Holy Spirit for being my closest and most intimate Friend and for the adventures you successfully have taken me on, revealing your power to thousands of people now and thousands forever more to come.

Table Of Contents

Introduction 1
Knowing Your Human Spirit 5
Redemption Of The Human Spirit 12
Nurturing The Human Spirit Of A Child 15
Mastering The Human Spirit 26
Stop Being Noisy 39
Life With "The Advantage" 49
The Seal 67
Dimensions 74
Bilingual 89
Waiting To Exhale 104
The Finishing Anointing 111
   Knowing Gifts 112
   Speaking Gifts 112
   Power 113
Epilogue 125

INTRODUCTION

What is the one thing that gives a person advantage in our culture today? It is wealth reckoned in terms of money. This opens doors and gives access to opportunity, information, posture and position in our society. Everyone who has obtained a measure of wealth, and lives in the affluent zone of life, walks with a certain boldness and confidence that the moment you meet them, you'll recognize they see themselves with leverage others don't have.

I have been around many affluent and wealthy people. It does not matter what country, state, city or continent I am in. Wealth gives people an advantage over gender, skin color, race, religious preferences and every other hindrance that may stop you and me from gaining entrance into certain arenas. What would you do right now if you had all the wealth you ever needed? How would you walk? How would you talk? How would you face your day? Would you carry yourself with a certain confidence, knowing you'll never have to worry about being in debt another day of your life? How would your wealth position you in society? Would it seat you in certain rooms at certain tables?

In our current American culture, we see the haves and the have-nots. Whether you want to admit it or not, the caste system of India, the segregation of the south, the bigotry of the north, the exclusion in religious circles, the rejection to education—are all tendered upon the advantage of wealth. People with wealth don't fear cultural norms or boundaries. They believe that their wealth gives them an advantage. They don't go through the same doors. They don't park in the same parking spaces. They are often ushered to the front and the top, and given leverage that we, who don't have the same economic or financial balance sheet, don't even know about. We sit way in the back of the same basketball game or in the top tier of a stadium because we bought cheap seat tickets. The nosebleed section is usually not even recognized by those in the box seats. They are closer to the court. They see the game clearly. They meet the athletes and oftentimes are invited to their homes. Personal relationships that span charitable opportunities, social functions arise. While we, who sit in the nosebleed section, can barely make it to our cars without a stampede. We are at a disadvantage simply because we did not buy suite tickets to the event, which cost thousands of dollars on an annual basis.

We saw the game. We heard the same songs. We saw the teams score, and we saw them win or lose. However, our vantage point was very different—based on our wealth. As much as I hate to admit it, even in the church, wealth can be used as an advantage for some. It's used to build the church, to help the pastor's vision, to add the educational addition and even sponsor disadvantaged young people for scholarships. When you have money, you can help many people. There is not a pastor or religious leader that I know of, who does *not* desire at least a portion of his or her parish to have wealth. While we love the flock, we must feed the flock. It takes money, lots of money to do great ministry work. The gospel is free. Jesus paid it all. That is what we say. But at the end of every service, we all go to count what came in through tithes and offerings because we still have bills to pay. Where there is no provision for the vision, the visionary suffers.

So, this advantage, in the natural, is tangible and seen. It's known and highly respected. So, what advantage do the rest of us have that has not yet acquired this level of affluence? Has God considered us in any way? Does He see the disadvantage that we, who are average wage earners, are at in our culture today? Is there something or someone that is available to us who lived by faith, literally, who we can use to position ourselves above the level of mediocrity?

I want to introduce to you the greatest gift given to us after salvation. Jesus said, *"It is for your advantage that I go away so that Holy Spirit can come."* For many years, I've been in ministry and the marketplace but have never had great personal wealth. I have preached in 39 nations, on 7 continents, and only God could have opened those doors. As a woman in ministry leadership, some would consider me a success because I have broken many barriers. I have laid a foundation for many women who aspire to be used of God despite religious bigotry. I've had successful businesses, and I've helped others start their businesses as a personal coach and consultant.

Yet, I've never done it with money. I've never done any of this with money. But when I was introduced to Holy Spirit, and intimately got to know Him for myself, I found out that He was the genius mind of God who knew everything about everything. If I asked Him, He would whisper the mysteries and secrets in my ear. Many times, I would look around a room and wonder how I got there. How did I get to this table? Why are they asking me what I think? Why are social political, thought leaders, influencers and business leaders consulting with me about life decisions? Why did they rely upon me and my wisdom and influence? Truly, God gave me the advantage when He gave me Holy Spirit. If He did it for me, He will do it for you.

Every morning of my life, for the last 45 years, I wake up with one statement:

"Good morning, Holy Spirit!" When I begin my day, talking to Holy Spirit and engaging Him in my daily journey, He deposits and downloads the very mind of God, favor, opportunity and access. He has navigated my way for more than 50 years. I can truly say that without money and wealth, I have lived an amazing life—all because of the advantage. Take this journey with me now as I guide you into a life-changing relationship and intimacy through intentional fellowship with God the Holy Spirit.

Knowing Your Human Spirit

In lieu of the two thoughts of evolution versus creation, this book starts from the premise that we were created by a higher being that had an intent and purpose that we would be like Him. How does the creation of man resemble the Creator? The Trinity represents God as three persons—one as the Father, who is the originator or the source; the Son—who preexisted with Him as Christ; and the Spirit—who is a person and who is responsible for the manifestation of the designs of the Father, which are administered through the Son. God's spirit is active in them all. The Son, Christ, is seen as the Word spoken by the Father. **John 1:1** says, *In the beginning was the Word, and the Word was with God, and the Word was God.* The Father is seen as the source of the design or pattern of everything created within the world's systems...the elements, the sun, the moon and stars. However, the most pivotal component of creations is not seen in the earth's designs, the sciences or the universe. It is seen when He now creates a being that is in His image and after His likeness.

Made out of the dirt, unlike anything else that He has created, His real creativity is shown in His creation of man. **Genesis 2:7** says, *And the Lord God formed man of the dust of the ground and breathed into his nostrils the breath of life and man became a living being.* This is a picture of a master craftsman shaping something like a work of art. Although man was made from the dirt, his value didn't come from the dirt. His value was not determined by what he was made out of. But how many of us value the body more? The value didn't come from the components of the dirt. The quality comes from what went into man—which was the breath of life. His value was not derived from the dirt, although, we tend to think that the dirt is where our true worth and advantage is— which is why we live at such a disadvantage.

The worth and value is found in the *ruach*, the breath of life, which is spirit. Now man's value increases. His human spirit now makes him compatible for fellowship, communion and worship. This created 'being' 'man' lying on the ground without any sense of smell, sight, love or companionship had no sense of pain, sorrow, nor the ability to think or create. It was simply dirt until the *ruach*, the breath, was put into him; now, he is capable of performing the assignment of dominion.

What is this *ruach* that has come from the Creator? From a nursing perspective, the respiratory starts with the nose, not the mouth. This is why God breathed into the nostrils of man and not the mouth. He went to the origin of the respiratory system. When we perform CPR, we breathe into the mouth. But we are not the originator of the breath of life. At the point of CPR, we are attempting to restore that which God has already placed inside of the body. God starts man breathing by breathing into his nostrils. Man takes his first breath and becomes a living being, a thinking being, a being of will and choice.

In the human respiratory system, air enters into the nostrils and then passes through the nasopharynx and oral pharynx through the glottis into the trachea, into the right and left bronchi, which branches and re-branches into the bronchioles. We think our mouth is our source of breathing. Your mouth is not a part of the respiratory system. It is part of the gastrointestinal system. However, it's the quickest way to get air into the lungs in trauma. That's why God didn't breathe into man's mouth. He breathed into his nostrils the breath of life so that it did not go into the abdominal cavity. The mouth is for eating and digesting food, it's not how you breathe. What also happened when God breathed the breath of life, this being became a living soul.

Very few people are aware that the value of life is in the breath that was given to us by God. The *ruach*, or breath, is spirit in the Hebrew. Because it came directly from God, it's what makes us the object of His affection or attention. The body returns back to the dirt at time of death. But our spirit leaves our body to return back to God. Contrary to popular opinion, our real worth is not in our achievements, our drives, our emotions or our experiences—our spirit, the invisible part of us, is where the real value lies. It is so protected and sealed off, that not only are we most times unaware of our spirit, but it also cannot be traumatized or compromised by any external event, hence our self-esteem is never damaged by life's ups and downs. Sometimes, a life event has so traumatized an individual; they become defined by the event and call themselves broken, ugly, and unvalued because some external stimuli went wrong. But if we develop this way of thinking in regards to the value that God gave us is internal, we'd know nothing ever devalues us. Our human spirit is always protected. Maybe our soul (mind, will and emotions) has been damaged. So, you must tap into your own human spirit so the area of the soul will dominate and not compromise your purpose and your success.

You are much more than a soul. You are more than a body. You are a spirit. You have a soul. You live in a body. Your worth and value are in how you develop and nurture your own human spirit. It's so powerful that by having knowledge of your human spirit, you can overcome any obstacle and bring your soul (mind, will and emotions) into subjection to a greater source of creativity. So many people are broken, hurting, in therapy and in counseling; medicating themselves with habits, religion and drugs, trying to make the soul get well while the human spirit lies ignored, suppressed and even silenced. Your spirit is on mute. It is waiting on you to activate it and again bring life to you. In hospital rooms around the world, I have seen trauma, injury, accidents and violence. Some injuries are life-threatening. All that medical science and practice provides is limited to the dirt (outer man). We try to insert intravenous solutions. We hydrate and offer medications, and our patients still don't recover.

But what I've seen are those who have nurtured and developed a relationship with God's spirit and their human spirit being in fellowship; no matter the trauma or the injury to the dirt man, the recovery rate is always higher. While a person who is broken in spirit, recovery rate is extremely low. There is invincibility in the human spirit that transcends science, statistics and schooling, which produces great results...healing and recovery. Even if the individual can respond to stimuli of happy music, verbal encouragement and prayer, as a nurse, I have seen them recover from life-threatening trauma. On the other hand, I have seen patients come in with little to nothing wrong. But because of a sad, broken spirit, with all the medication and technology available, health is never obtained.

Human spirit is powerful. It is a direct connection to the supernatural. It is sensitive to supernatural sound, faith, leading and direction. Your human spirit is smarter than your educational development. There is a perception that when developed, the human spirit will always provide incredible options that are limited in education. Some people call it intuition. Knowing that it is available, oftentimes we yet rely upon the dirt manor emotions; we totally ignore our perception and trample on its ability to prevent long-term consequences. Human spirit, when nurtured properly, operates as a receiver to a very potent satellite. There are always messages downloaded. There are always signals. Frequency is never lost. We are either not perceptive or receptive and defy what we have received from the satellite. We end up in lifetime therapy and support groups with out-of-control emotions, terrible tempers and tantrums, until we come back again to that ground and begin again with our Creator. For the purpose of our dialog, we shall call this experience being *born again*, not in the outer man, nor in the soulish man (intellect, emotions, and will)—but in our human spirit. Being born again gives a fresh life to our human spirit.

The weight of life needs no agreement from our soulish man, its heavy enough. Life by itself, with all the twists and turns, can leave anyone a victim helpless and hopeless, without remedy. God, in His infinite wisdom, knew we would need a force greater than life that would sustain us and elevate us above life itself. Adam put all of us in trouble by following his emotions and not trusting the breath. He doubted the voice of the breath. He second guessed himself into treason and broken communion. His spirit man is now ex-communicated from the daily talks and walks with his Creator. He now has to make it by the sweat of his brow. He now has to make his own life work for him and his family. The signal has been compromised. The Creator (the source, the satellite) still has much to say to His created being. But now, Adam's human spirit is dead and can no longer receive the frequency. He is left to a menial life instead of dominating. His human spirit is no longer the focus. Now, he must focus on the dirt man. Now, he has shame and guilt. Now, his being is suffering and struggling, and he ended up in a mess without communion with the satellite. Intuition is compromised.

When this happens to you, your perception is dull. Your appetite is wrong. You are driven by the lust of the eye, lust of the flesh and the pride of life. Everything, God never wanted us to struggle with becomes our ambition. We needed redemption. We needed a savior.

Our human spirit needed a second chance.

Redemption of the Human Spirit

In Christian theology, redemption is an element of salvation that means deliverance from sin. It is the act of buying back something, or paying a price to return something to one's possession. In ancient times, it often refers to the act of buying a slave. The Christian use of redemption is that someone, through His sacrifice of death, purchased humankind from slavery to set us free from the bondage of disobedience. The Greek word for redemption is *agorazo*, which means to purchase. Another word for redemption is *exagorazo*. Redemption always involves going from something to something else. In this case, it is going from darkness into light, from silence into sound, from hopelessness into freedom. **Ephesians 1:7-8**, *In Him we have redemption through his blood, the forgiveness of sins, in accordance with the riches of God's grace that He lavished on us with all wisdom and understanding.*

The third Greek word connected with redemption is *lutroo*, which means to obtain release by the payment of a price. The price in Christianity was precious blood, obtaining our release from sin, which He sacrificed. It was for the entire world, not just for one group of people. Christ actually came to redeem all of humanity out of their bondage to the dirt. It is the dirt component that gives us such a disadvantage. We have so many limitations and no means of reparation to make amends for our mistakes, those committed by us, and those done to us. Therefore, redemption is vital. Because of our human spirit being rendered dead in the Garden of Eden, we lost focus. The drive of life has made everything else more important. But because of the work of Jesus Christ, we now can go back to Eden and live on top of the world: God's original intent was where communion and fellowship equaled peace and joy not thorns and thistles.

By faith, we must receive the finished work of Christ and accept Him as our kinsman redeemer. Restoring our human spirit back to its original state while still in the earthly realm is a major advantage given to us. We should be grateful for the rest of our lives. When we receive Christ, that which was dead now comes alive, and God's original intent is restored.

Ephesians 2:1-3, *And you He made alive who was dead in trespasses and sins, in which you once walked according to the course of this world, according to the prince of the power of the air, the spirit who now works in the sons of disobedience, among whom also we all once conducted ourselves in the lust of our flesh, fulfilling the desire of the flesh and of the mind, and were by nature children of wrath, just as the others.*

The kindness of God, manifested through Jesus, will now make you alive in your human spirit. The valuable part of you is now able to soar and succeed in life in spite of whatever comes your way. When you experience the kindness and mercy of Jesus Christ, you are now restored back to the place of dominion. But, you still have work to do in *knowing* your human spirit and nurturing this vital part of your being to hear once again the sound of its Creator.

Nurturing the Human Spirit of a Child

Acts 2:17 says, *And it shall come to pass in the last days, saith God, I will pour out of my Spirit upon all flesh: and your sons and your daughters shall prophesy.*

Acts 2:39 says, *For the promise is unto you, and to your children, and to all that are afar off, even as many as the Lord our God shall call.*

At what age does a child exhibit their independence and need to be free? How early do you recognize the inner strength of a child? How many parents have the tendency to modify that strength through disciplinary actions rather than developing and encouraging that inner strength in that child? Recognizing early on, a child's human spirit is key to training the child in the way he or she should go. However, because we most likely are unfamiliar with our own human spirit, parents seek to break the spirit of a child, not understanding that it is at these early ages where the human spirit is most innocent and most powerful.

The Bible gives parents the responsibility of teaching children, and teaching must involve more than academics. Parents must find the time and the information for investing in their child based upon the predisposition of the child's spirit. At an early age, nurturing a child's human spirit is so important if we want that child to be an effective, Godly adult. It is absolutely possible by nurturing a child's human spirit that the child, at a very early age, will have a taste for spiritual things and will avoid catastrophes as he/she ages—therefore, avoiding rebellion, defiance and disobedience. The gifts of a child are realized very early. These gifts are deposited in the child's spirit before birth. The child's career, preferences for a mate, future career choices, likes and dislikes, are already in the DNA of the child's spirit. Guided conversations with observations will help a parent mold the child according to the DNA of the human spirit.

As a child, I was very precocious. I was smart. I was involved. I was very communicative and inquisitive. I had good understanding of things that went on around me. By the age of three, I was able to read. By the age of four, I was able to play songs on the piano that I heard. It was during these early years that I was also introduced to the voice of God. I was very interested in creation—flowers, the stars, the sun, the sky and even water. I had a lot of questions. I sat down at the piano at the age of four and was able to play a complete hymn with one finger. My mother heard me and immediately purchased a piano for our home. She nurtured my human spirit. I played the piano all day and all evening. I didn't want to watch a lot of TV because it was limited. Even though radio was prominent, I was fascinated by the sound of my fingers touching the keys. Sometimes I sang.

Sometimes I cried. I touched God very early. He touched me very early.

My mother watched me play and sang along while I played. I could remember the tunes from the Sunday services and Sunday school. I always ran home and played them on my piano. I couldn't yet read music, but my ear was perfect. Remember, I was only four. One day, I was at my mother's beauty shop, which was in the home, on a Saturday and I was playing and singing with the other children who were there with their parents. They were my captive audience. I turned my piano bench around, placed the music book on the bench in front of me, and shared a message of hope. It was so powerful all of the customers, along with my mother, came in the hallway and stood behind me. I felt it. It was so real. The other children were captivated because they did not play. They didn't giggle. This moment lasted about 15 minutes. In this basement daycare, in the front of a beauty salon, my first sermon was preached at the age of four.

I heard a client say, "Corletta is so gifted. She is going to preach and sing." My mother said, "Yes, I know. So I must prepare her for it." I am ever so grateful that my mom knew it was her responsibility to nurture my human spirit. That scenario could have gone very differently. For many children, what parents or caregivers see in a child is often put under restraints, condemnation and correction or exposed to sheer cruelty. A loud child is not a bad child; it's a child who has something to say. A quiet child is not an introvert;

that child is a child who is listening. A child who is rambunctious and has a lot of energy cannot be constrained to a chair or a room. The child's human spirit is already programmed. As parents, and members of the community, instead of constraining or being critical of a child's human spirit, we must be perceptive and listen to our human spirit of how to properly handle the child. If not, there will be conflict early on between the parent and the child. The child will seek freedom and the caregiver will exercise restraint. The child will desire to speak, and the caregiver will take away their voice.

This is how people grow up and get into the wrong career and into the wrong lane for success and prosperity. Early on, their purpose was not identified or appreciated. The characteristics of a child, early on, require the parent to know how God designed the child. In **Luke 2:52**, Jesus, as a 12-year-old child, "grew in wisdom" intellectually and in stature. He also grew in favor with God spiritually and with man, he grew socially and emotionally.

What are the age level characteristics and needs of a child *from birth to five years old*? Children develop at different rates in different areas, and we must always treat them as individuals. We must know why a child has been born and given to a particular home and set of parents. The absence of discernment can kill a child's human spirit. This child needs love, kindness and a listening ear. A child's senses are very sensitive and alert. There is a love for repetition and routine. This child is very imaginative even though their knowledge and vocabulary are limited. They'll ask many questions, and you should answer them all and not ignore them. They are very individualistic and always demand attention.

In these early ages, a child is imitative. Proper examples of conduct—attitude, practices, and conversation—is vital. The emotional and spiritual aspects of a child from ages 0-5 require our attention because they are very affectionate. We must direct them to the Lord and to positive reinforcement about God and His love for them. A child is awakening spiritually and already has a natural trust, with simple faith. A child is filled with awe and wonder and is very sensitive to spiritual atmospheres. Guarding the environment of a child at these early ages from fear, negativity, condemnation and sarcasm is vital. Their environment should be calm, loving and Christ-like. They are very impressionable and teachable. *Teach nothing at this age that has to be unlearned.* They should always feel secure and live in an atmosphere where they know they are loved. It needs to be reinforced over and over again.

This is the time to introduce a child to the language of God the Father, God the Son and God the Holy Spirit. We must ask the child often if they can hear God and if they are listening to Him. Teach them the simplicity of prayer—how to talk to God and how to listen to Him. This will take them a long way in the course of their life. The mental capacity of a child between these ages, *and slightly older at four, five and six,* although immature, wants to do more than it's capable of. So, we must furnish the things for the child to be able to understand. Explain slowly and clearly. Never rush. Clarify over and over again, with a simple routine with limited choices. Because they ask countless questions, answer them honestly. But seek the reasons behind the questions. Encourage them to listen to their human spirit.

Do not give the impression that their inquiry is stupid. Do not repress their imagination. Use concrete terms, avoid symbolism and help them to distinguish between fact and fantasy. Lead them to activities that increase their ability to be perceptive. Give them an opportunity to talk. In their talking, they will tell you what they are hearing. *This is the age of innocence. Keep them safe. Keep them from molestation and violation.* Keep the environment pure. Create space for confidence. Help them to be socially involved with others. Encourage leadership activities. Provide dolls and toys to play with and illustrate Bible stories. Always share with them that they can talk with you about anything. Let them know that not only are *you* listening, but *God* is listening as well and is interested in what they have to say. Children are full of wonder. We must stimulate their desire to worship. Even if they can't read well, encourage audio and visual means of Bible stories so they can learn the language of spirit. This requires time, patience and understanding of the child. But it will produce a very sensitive, mature adult who avoids many tragedies and life-altering consequences because they were trained to hear their human spirit.

Teach them to do right and teach them the joy of doing right. Teach them obedience and, from time to time, ask them what they hear. Ask them what their inner self is saying. Ask them why they do the things they do. Check often to see who is influencing the human spirit of your child. This child is born for greatness. If you nurture their human spirit, you will see greatness evolve.

Around the ages of 9-11, your child is at the age of accountability. Right and wrong is clear. At this age, they can accept more responsibility. Emotionally and spiritually, they can be quick-tempered and even selfish. They also recognize sin as sin. Their innocence is quickly waning. The soul (emotions, will, intellect) fights for domination along with the changes in the physical body, hormones and peer pressure. The soul is now the strongest voice and the challenge of purity is at hand. Purity is at stake--not just of the body, but of their emotions, their appetites, what they are attracted to and their concern about relationships. Because the soul now is becoming so powerful and dominant, you observe defiance and deliberate disobedience to commands and expectations. Depending upon outside stimuli, the child may become sassy or may become totally silent. Both of these models indicate that the soul is taking over.

If the caregivers are alert, they will challenge and channel the behavior and the actions of the child. This is where redemption must be introduced for some and reintroduced for other children who accepted Christ at an early age. They need to know Christ frees us from the penalty of sin. We must connect the child to a more mature flow of consequences and choices. Set high standards, biblical standards and good moral standards. We must live in front of them deliberate, Godly lives. The child now is ready to make a mature emotional decision about Christ and His ways. Now, the child becomes accountable for acts of disobedience. As they enter this age category, they must be given stronger and stiffer boundaries—not to break their spirit—but to corral the insistent loud sound of their soul. This is where the child must be given the opportunity to make decisions and be held responsible for those decisions.

This is where appetites of the soul and emotional stimuli of the soul rise. This is the age where we lose most of our children. Although they may not have the tools or resources at this point to rebel, rebellion is in their hearts. But if you have been treating the child as God's creation with a human spirit, making the shift back from the soul to the spirit won't be difficult. If you have ignored the human spirit of this child, the next few years will be a time of intense conversations, lawlessness, rebellion and emotional collapse in the home. Now, this child, without knowledge of their human spirit development or Christ, is at a disadvantage that may last until adulthood. Stop and look at where your children are. If they are still in your home, begin immediately to cultivate and redirect your child. It was never God's intent for our soul to create disrepair and do permanent damage at this early age. Stop now and get in touch with your own human spirit. Get in touch with Holy Spirit and bring your child out of the darkness of the soul's dominion into clarity and light of living with the advantage of their human spirit, which is connected to God's spirit. It will guide them the rest of their days.

Children are lost at this age. They are lost sexually, mentally and emotionally. If there has been any form of abuse—verbal, physical or emotional—this is the time to correct it while the child still has a tender heart. If the child has been violated, get professional help. If the child has been ignored, stop and pay attention. If you have been too busy to pour into your child, or you took the child in a wrong direction, turn it around now so the child's greatness and purpose can be realized. The ages of 9-11 years old are not too late. It's not too late for this child to have the advantage. If this child is not being raised in a God-fearing home, this is where a village comes into play.

A child still has greatness. If the immediate environment that a child resides in does not nurture the child, the village can still play a pivotal role—aunts, uncles, cousins, mentors, teachers, pastors and family friends. These people are still important in the life of the child. If you are a grandparent or aunt, neighbor or friend, grab the child and speak life into the child. Speak over the child words of life. Speak greatness over that child. Give that child every advantage and introduce them to Holy Spirit as soon as possible. For this promise of Holy Spirit is for our children. Don't ignore your child's spirituality. Don't ignore your spiritual responsibility. Don't say it cannot be done. There is not a child that is born that is not a candidate for greatness—a candidate for The Advantage.

These things must be considered when nurturing the human spirit of a child:

- ❖ A child needs love.
- ❖ A child needs security.
- ❖ A child needs acceptance.
- ❖ A child needs discipline (self-control).
- ❖ A child needs independence.
- ❖ A child needs recognition of worth.

The following are practical methods of nurturing a child's human spirit:

- ❖ Artistic Activities—Children can learn God's Word through art.

- ❖ Drama Activities—These activities link the child's imagination and emotions to the Bible. It can make the Bible come alive.

- ❖ Oral Communication—Most children enjoy talking and sharing their ideas and experiences.

- ❖ Creative Writing—When you see a child writing on a wall, or coloring on your walls and mirrors at home, pay attention. You may have an author on your hands.

❖ **Music Activities—Music can be used to teach children worship and it encourages them to respond to God.**

❖ **Research Activities—These are the children who can read for hours, but it needs to be guided. Buy these children maps, dictionaries and encyclopedias. Give them research incentives.**

❖ **Bible Games—Children love to play and learn. Use games to assist the child in remembering specific truths about God, Jesus and Holy Spirit.**

Guidance and encouragement can keep your children motivated and nurtured. Simple adjustments in the home's environment will give children a long healthy, mental, social, physical and spiritual life.

Now this is The Advantage!

Mastering the Human Spirit

In order to fully appreciate The Advantage, and His presence in your life, let's examine where The Advantage actually takes up residence. We are created in the image of God tri unity. We are spirit, with a soul, and we live in a body. Let's break these areas down. The human spirit is what was given to us by our Creator to connect us back to Him. It came from Him as He breathed into man's nostrils the breath of life. The term *ruach*, often referenced in the Old Testament, means breath, wind or spirit. Our Creator is spirit. He made us spirit to be compatible for a relationship with Him. The very breath that is in our nostrils indicates spirit is present and alive within us. Our nose only functions as a receptor for air or oxygen. But the moment that spirit leaves the body, our nose will cease to function and breathe in air. Breathing is an indicator of spirit being alive within us. Our true selves created in the image and likeness of God is spirit. This is our human spirit. This is where communion begins. This is where fellowship originates. Our human spirit is responsible for navigating, much like a GPS system—connected to the larger satellite. Our human spirit receives signals. Our human spirit must be developed and cultivated to pick up the signals easily. With our human spirit, we perceive, discern and know things beyond the mind or the intellect. Some people call it a gut feeling or premonition. We've called it déjà vu. All of these indicate that we are spiritual beings having a human experience. God, in His wisdom, then gave us a soul.

The soul is defined as the principle of life, feeling, thought and action in humans. Regarded as a distinct entity separate from the body, and commonly held to be separable in existence from the body; it is known as intellect or mind, volition or will, emotions, wants and desires. This part of us, the soul, was never intended to guide us or rule us. This part of us is at the deepest level, the very base of us. I know you put a lot of emphasis on your thought life, your mind, emotions and will—and we would love for this part of us to be celebrated. But it was God's original intent that our human spirit would lead us, and our soul would conform to the leading of our human spirit—communicating its desires and activities through our body. Our physical body is never to be in charge; it was to be the servant of our soul, as our soul was the servant to our human spirit. But something happened, and this went dreadfully wrong.

In the Garden of Eden, something went dreadfully wrong. God gave Adam His first commandment of what to do—and what not to do. He said to him in **Genesis 2:16**, *"You are free to eat from any tree in the garden. But you must not eat from the tree of the knowledge of good and evil, for when you eat of it, you shall surely die."* This is where the trouble began. Adam did not obey God. The very tree he was told not to eat from, because he had volition and choice, he made a decision to go against what God spoke to him. Immediately, confusion broke out. Now, instead of spirit communing with God, it now runs from God and hides from God. Adam ate from the tree of the knowledge of good and evil, and this is the beginning of mixture. This is what confuses most of us—good and evil—especially when it comes together. The knowledge of good and evil is what God never wanted Adam to obtain—He only wanted him to know life, to know good, to know Him. On a daily basis, God Himself would come down to the Garden of Eden and commune with Adam—spirit to spirit. This is not Holy Spirit. This is Adam's human spirit. It was open and aware of God. His receptors were sharp. There was no confusion. He knew the voice of God. He knew where to meet God. He knew when God was coming and welcomed the fellowship. But the moment Adam disobeyed, he ran to hide himself. Even then, God looked for him; because it is God who wants to commune with us through our human spirit.

Even when there is a breach, God still looks for us. He finds us by our human spirit. But when we are out of order, our soul, our will, our logic kicks in and becomes the boss-introducing to us other ideas and options that take us away from God. The more our soul dominates our human spirit, the less sensitive our human spirit is to God. The Bible says, *before we met Christ, we were dead in trespasses and sin* **(Ephesians 2:1)**. We lived and followed the ways of this world. The ruler of the kingdom of the air who is now at work in those who are disobedient. All of us lived among them at one time, gratifying the cravings of our sinful nature and following its desires and thoughts. Like the rest, we were by nature, objects of wrath. What was dead? Our spirit. When Adam sinned against God, humanity came into the world. Every baby that is born is born dead. Yes, they're breathing. But their human spirit is not responsive yet. So now, the soul and the body work havoc in our lives and lead us into mischief. Many times, irreversible damage is done while we are in this state of our human spirit being asleep, dead. So, we become accustomed to the soul dominating and guiding us. It takes us on a journey that we don't even enjoy, but we have no help from our human spirit—until we find Christ and place our faith in Him. Immediately, upon hearing the gospel of Jesus Christ, believing it and accepting The Savior, our human spirit is quickened and made alive. For the first time in our lives since birth, our GPS system is back on track.

We were navigating by the soul—what we thought, what we felt, what we experienced. It was always about us. The soul doesn't know God and will never lead us to God. The soul is selfish and brutish and low down. It's dirty. Without our human spirit, we become accustomed to the soul being in the driver's seat. Our body will simply comply—and we blame the body for everything. We blame the devil. However, neither of these is responsible for the decisions we've made and the consequences we now have to live with. It was the soul all the time that kept us gratifying ourselves, our sinful natures. Do you see how vital your human spirit is? To live without your human spirit being alive, and connected to God, is like having a head without a brain. It's like having an automobile without an engine. You're lost. You're stuck. You're not going anywhere. We make tremendous advancements in life without ever engaging our human spirit.

So, we are not at all familiar with our human spirit once it is awakened. So, what now will we do? I've been dead all these years—driven by my soul, emotions and pain, and now my human spirit wants to commune with God— wanting to bring peace, joy and this new sphere of life. God, in His wisdom, says, *"You will need help to reconnect with me."* Jesus says, *"I must go away so the Comforter will come."* He comes to live in our human spirit. He is Resident God. **John 16:13-15** says, *But when he, the Spirit of truth, comes, he will guide you into all the truth. He will not speak on his own; he will speak only what he hears, and he will tell you what is yet to come. He will glorify me because it is from me that he will receive what he will make known to you. All that belongs to the Father is mine. That is why I said the Spirit will receive from me what he will make known to you."* He now is in our human spirit to guide and enhance, until our human spirit no longer responds to our soul's leadership. Holy Spirit helps us and gives us the advantage over our own souls. This is an amazing truth that while yes, we fight enemies without. Yes, we encounter principalities, challenges, problems, and even troubled people, but none of them pose the threat to our well-being like our own soul. Remember for most of your life, your soul has run your life.

Your own soul has been the nemesis. You carry a record that now Holy Spirit, with the help of the Word of God, must transform and rearrange, even with some files being deleted. This is The Advantage. Holy Spirit is our advantage over our terrible mistakes, trauma and tragedy. Without Holy Spirit, we will never be able to be free of guilt, shame and regret. Our soul carries the record and reminds us over and over again how we've failed, how we were violated and how we were mistreated. It reminds us how we didn't handle certain situations well. Who would want to live this life with just your soul, and no Holy Spirit? The soul is the hard drive. Now, through the living and breathing Word of God, our minds are transformed to be the new creation—living a supernatural, amazing life. All because Holy Spirit is resident and lives in our human spirit. Paul says, **(Romans 12:1-2)** *"Be not conformed to this world but be ye transformed by the renewing of your minds."* Paul also tells us, **(2 Corinthians 10:4-6)** *"The weapons we fight with are not the weapons of the world. On the contrary, they have divine power to demolish strongholds. We demolish arguments and every pretension that sets itself up against the knowledge of God, and we take captive every thought to make it obedient to Christ. And we will be ready to punish every act of disobedience, once your obedience is complete."*

So, our battle is the soul versus the spirit. Paul says, **Romans 7:15-20** *"I do not understand what I do. For what I want to do I do not do, but what I hate I do. And* *if I do what I do not want to do, I agree that the law is good. As it is, it is no longer I myself who do it, but it is sin living in me. For I know that good itself does not dwell in me, that is, in my sinful nature. For I have the desire to do what is good, but I cannot carry it out. For I do not do the good I want to do, but the evil I do not want to do—this I keep on doing. Now if I do what I do not want to do, it is no longer I who do it, but it is sin living in me that does it."* The continual battle is soul and spirit. How did I get like this? I lived without my human spirit being active in my life for so long, that my mind, will and emotions have been trained a certain way. Therefore, my human spirit is now awakened and is flooded with the love of God. But the warfare is real. So Holy Spirit is there within me, mediating the battle. He umpires the battle between soul and spirit. As I learn to hear and follow Holy Spirit, each victory over my soul makes my human spirit stronger. What once held me a prisoner, I now imprison. **Romans 7:22** says, *"For in my inner being I delight in God's law."* The law of God lives in my human spirit. My inner being loves God. The war is between my soul and members of my body. My body has served my soul for so long, I had to train my human spirit to submit to Holy Spirit. I gained the advantage over all of the vices, habits, appetites, desires and lusts that had me captive. Thanks be to God, through Jesus Christ, our Lord. I now can bring those thoughts into captivity and make them obey the Word of God that lives in my human spirit.

Is it easy? No. Is it possible? Yes. Is it worth fighting for? Absolutely yes! To live the life of the Spirit is a wonderful life. It's an amazing life. It doesn't take place overnight because you did not learn to do wrong overnight. There were multiple years of going in the opposite direction of God. But give yourself time and be diligent about it. Pray in the Holy Spirit. Read your Bible. Listen for instructions from God. Pay close attention to what Holy Spirit is saying to you. Little by little, you will go from victim to victor. You will become strong in faith, bold in your power and identity with Christ. It's an amazing life because you now have The Advantage.

There are three areas that you must be aware of with your new enlightened human spirit. The first area is **"Conviction."** Your convictions should be based upon the Word of God. What God says is good, what God says is evil, what God says He loves and what God says He hates. This should be the basis of our convictions. Our convictions reside in our human spirit. Once you develop your human spirit to merge with Holy Spirit, truth will be deposited in you. The truth of God's Word will be a delight to your life. Your convictions are shaped and should never be violated—even though there will be multiple opportunities for you to compromise. Never do it.

But be very careful that you don't confuse convictions with the next area, which is **"Conscience."** The area of convictions will be small. You may have four or five deep-seated Godly convictions. But in the area of your conscience, which is a much bigger space, there may be many things that you don't like and choose not to engage in. Remember, convictions are only for you and not for others. You can teach them to your children, but it doesn't have to become their convictions. We have to be careful that we don't judge people when they don't share our convictions. They should be very precious to us, even if others around us don't agree. We should never be forced to do anything beyond our convictions.

Our conscience gives us more liberty and freedom. In **1 Corinthians 8**, Paul discusses eating meat that was sacrificed to idols; there were those who were there who had strong convictions about eating the temple's meat as their regular food. That was their convictions. But there were those, who were there, that did not share those convictions. Their freedom became a stumbling block to those who were weak. Paul says to them, *"Don't eat the meat, even though you are free and have no convictions in this area because there are those around you who are weak."* They have not yet formed a conviction about it. They are struggling watching you eat it, while they are taught not to eat it. We may not have convictions about certain things, and we have more liberty because our conscience gives us permission. In these areas of consciousness, you must rely heavily upon Holy Spirit when it's appropriate and when it's not appropriate. While convictions should never be optional, certain matters of consciences are. You have to rely upon The Advantage to take you in and out of places, be in order, and not offensive. These are the areas of your consciousness.

For example, I like drinking wine. I have no conviction about drinking wine. I was raised on wine. My mother made wine. It was a celebration during Thanksgiving for my mom to bring out her new vat of wine. So, wine was a staple in our home. We had it with dinner. If we had a stomach ache, she gave it to us to settle our stomach. We never saw wine as a sin. However, as I moved about in certain faith communities, I discovered that to some, drinking wine is a sin and a deeply held conviction for them. But Holy Spirit helped me to understand, although it's lawful for me, it may not be expedient to partake of it in certain circles. **1 Corinthians 8:9-13** says, *"Be careful, however, that the exercise of your rights does not become a stumbling block to the weak. For if someone with a weak conscience sees you, with all your knowledge, eating in an idol's temple, won't that person be emboldened to eat what is sacrificed to idols? So, this weak brother or sister, for whom Christ died, is destroyed by your knowledge. When you sin against them in this way and wound their weak conscience, you sin against Christ. Therefore, if what I eat causes my brother or sister to fall into sin, I will never eat meat again, so that I will not cause them to fall."*

On a trip to Nigeria, I discovered that women wearing pants in their culture is offensive. It's a no-no. This is a cultural standard I was unaware of. Having traveled from America, I had women on my team who wore slacks on the plane. When we deplaned, I quickly picked up that something was wrong. Certain members of my team were being treated a certain way. When I looked around and gauged the situation, the most obvious thing was that these two women had on slacks. So, I went to them and said, "When you get your bags, change out of your slacks. I think we have hit a cultural restriction for women in slacks." Both of these women were strong Christians. I, as the team leader, had no idea that this was inappropriate attire for women in this country. One lady agreed right away. The other one wanted to defy the status quo. She said point blank, "I'm not changing my pants." I appealed. I apologized to her for not knowing and forewarning her, especially since I don't wear pants a lot. I obliged her to put on a skirt when she got her luggage. She still told me she would not change. I don't think this was a matter of conviction as much as defiance. As we proceeded through the airport, she was molested on every side; the police bothered her, and immigration officers detained her. Her baggage was inspected over and over again. Ultimately, after three hours of inquisition, we finally left the airport. When we arrived at the hotel, she was visibly angry. She wanted to return back to the United States. I said to her, "All you had to do was change your pants."

Because it offended the cultural location area where we were in, she should have taken them off. This is an area where Holy Spirit will help us. We are responsible for respecting the convictions of others, not just our own. This is where Paul says, *"I become all things to all people that I might win them to Christ."*

The final area is the area of **"Preference."** We must master this area and understand that by this being the widest area of the dictates of our life, in certain situations, our preferences may or may not be driven by the Word. It could be the way we were raised, childhood rules and regulations, and not necessarily good for all. Every family has their preferences. Even in cooking—not everyone makes chicken the same way. We have our preferences. But in developing and mastering your human spirit, we must not be picky with our preferences. Not at any time should we pass judgment on someone who does not adhere to our preferences. If we can only abide in peace in our families, on our jobs, in our churches, or wherever we go, this is the ultimate goal.

As you develop a relationship with Holy Spirit in your human spirit, you will be able to readily detect your convictions, your consciences and your preferences. These are the boundaries of your life. Preference will change. Consciousness will be fluid from time to time. But your convictions are steadfast and built upon the Word of God. Allow Holy Spirit to speak truth to you in every situation. Listen intently to the still small voice. Govern your lives accordingly.

One of the ways I have navigated, in my life, staying in touch with Holy Spirit is through worship. My devotional time with God is most precious. When I worship God privately and publicly, my human spirit is developing fellowship with God. In **John 4**, Jesus tells us the Father is seeking those who worship Him in spirit and truth. That word spirit is small s—meaning it is my spirit that worships. If you go back to the beginning of this chapter, I shared that it was always God's intent for us to commune with Him spirit to spirit. Our Father is still looking for the human spirit that is filled with truth to worship Him. This is the only part of us that is compatible with God. If you want to grow in the area of your convictions, in your conscience, clearly define your preferences, having victory over limitations; then worship is a powerful key to hearing Holy Spirit more clearly.

It is the one practice of our faith that engages our human spirit and creates a bond of love between us and God. When you really love God, you will obey God and quickly respond having the Advantage speak to you.

Worship is intimacy between a believer and God, much like sexual intercourse is intimacy between a husband and a wife. It creates the oneness of mind and dialogue, ideas and goals. The more you worship, the more you master your human spirit. The more attentive your spirit will be to the leading and guiding of Holy Spirit.

Monitor and master your human spirit.

Stop Being Noisy

So many people spend their lifetime wandering aimlessly. They don't have direction. They don't know what they really want to do, where they really want to go, or how to get there. Even those who know they are in the earth for purpose, with purpose, on purpose usually have no idea of their God-given purpose... that reason, that main thing they were created to accomplish. Many people think it's enough to be saved, but it's not. Salvation is for eternal life after one passes away from the earth. But for direction, for help, for strategy one must have The Advantage. One must have Holy Spirit!

In this day and age, many automobiles come with a Global Positioning System (GPS). In addition, the cell phones we use today allow us to map and navigate through life, right from the palms of our hands at the push of a button. So, if we're lost and we don't know how to get home, or we're going to a destination we've never visited before, we simply plug in the address and we get both a visible map and audible step-by-step guide. Even if we make a mistake and make the wrong turn or take the wrong exit, the navigation system realizes we are off track and redirects us. It's calculated and precise. If you only have 200 feet before you need to make a turn, it tells you, "In 200 feet, make a right turn." Even when you arrive at your destination, it announces to you, "You have arrived at your destination. The route guidance is now finished." Whereas in the past, we've used maps and an atlas for road trips and directions, now—no matter where we are—our phone or our built-in GPS system can direct us and put us back on track. Some navigational systems even mute or lower the music when it needs to update the driver on the next move because, at this point, it's more important that you hear the next direction and instruction than listen to music or continue a phone call.

Likewise, Holy Spirit is our guide. He is our navigational system. He's right there, daily, waiting to lead us, push us, pull us back or reposition us. He's there to tell us when to yield or pause. He's there to help us differentiate when we need to simply stop and when we have the green light to move forward. He is our built-in GPS! But what happens when you feel lost and you don't hear Holy Spirit? What do you do when you feel like He's ignoring you or He's simply on break?

John 10:4-5 says: *When he has brought out all his own, he goes on ahead of them, and his sheep follow him because they know his voice. But they will never follow a stranger; in fact, they will run away from him because they do not recognize a stranger's voice.* In this passage of Scripture, we recognize a few things. Holy Spirit, our guide, our Shepherd, always goes ahead of us. He lives both in the present, walking with us daily, and yet, far into the future. So, nothing surprises Him. Nothing moves Him to fear or shocks Him. And because He is already where we are trying to get to, we have to follow His lead. We can't make it to our next destination on our own will and knowledge. We follow His lead by listening to His voice. Just like your mother and father have a distinct voice, Holy Spirit has a distinct voice. Even if you played outside as a child with a group of children, when a mother called for her child to come inside, you knew if it was your mother's voice or not. Likewise, we are the sheep—we are the children—of Holy Spirit. And His children know His voice. So, if we find ourselves in a season where we don't know what to do next and we feel lost, it's not that we don't know Holy Spirit's voice per se. Perhaps, we need to simply silence some of the noise this life can bring on a day-to-day basis.

Noise is defined as irregular fluctuations that accompany a transmitted electrical signal but are not part of it and tend to obscure it. So, noise can come in various forms and mediums. Daily, we're inundated with alerts, updates, posts, texts and tags. We're consumed with our to-do lists, our packed schedules, meetings and phone-calls. We're raising children, tending to spouses, running businesses and trying to maintain some form of a social life with friends and colleagues. We've got hundreds of emails we need to sift through daily, programs and strategies we need to implement, and somewhere in the midst of all that—we need to eat and sleep.

But rarely do we schedule a meeting with Holy Spirit. When do we set aside time to find out what *He* wants us to do, not what we think is the next best thing to do. When do we commune with Him? We hit the ground running, from the time our feet hit the floor in the morning, until we lay our head back on that same pillow to rest—only to do it all over again the very next day. Days, weeks, even months go by and we soon realize that we're wandering aimlessly when in fact, we don't have to. Holy Spirit wants nothing more than to commune with us, like He did with Adam in the Garden of Eden. He wants to communicate with us. He wants to direct, guide and lead us—not just in the big decisions we make—but the small, minute, everyday decisions we make. But if we can't hear Him, if we can't decipher His voice aside from the noise, we get distracted. We get sidetracked. We lose focus and momentum. And even if we minimize the external distractions, the noise from the hustle and bustle of everyday life, we're still oftentimes faced with some of our biggest battles— which ironically, come from within.

Even when we know we heard God, we know what Holy Spirit said and told us to do, sometimes we simply *don't*. We *don't* follow instructions. We *don't* take heed to the warnings He sends right before we walk into a trap of some sort. We just *don't*. We talk ourselves out of what Holy Spirit said, what He promised and even when He may have shown us. We doubt His promises because they don't happen instantly. We question the validity of our gifting and callings. We shrink back in fear. We lay down our harps of praise and wallow in self-pity. Over time, the noise of self-doubt, self-pity and fear steal our hope. Suddenly, we're spiritually paralyzed—we can't move forward to the left or to the right because we don't believe the promises, the teachings and the principles Holy Spirit outlined for us in the Word of God. We don't believe them, and half of the time, our thoughts, our vision and our hearing are so clouded that we don't remember them in totality.

You've heard the analogy of the two shoulder angels, on one shoulder there's the good angel, who is clothed in white, and represents our conscience. On the other shoulder, there's the bad angel, who is often clothed in red with a pitchfork, and represents the devil who brings temptation. Many psychologists use this image to depict the inner conflict of one's character. It's a constant internal battle. On the one shoulder, you have instruction from your angelic representative. On the other, you have instruction from dark, demonic forces that contradict everything you've just heard from your angelic representative.

Likewise, Satan is always looking for a crack, a small hole, a little slit to slither his way into the minds and habits of the believer. He'll tell you God isn't going to come through and he doesn't care about you. He'll tell you this is the end and there is nothing greater than this—your life will be just like it is in this day, this moment, this hour. He can't kill you, so his tactic is to make the believer quit, give up and throw in the towel before he or she receives the promise of the Father. He seeks to discourage you from birth because he knows if you ever find out your true, authentic purpose—who you are in Christ and the power you possess—you'll be unstoppable. No matter what he whispers in your ear or tries to tempt you with, you'll be strong in the Lord, trusting in the power of Holy Spirit's might!

1 Peter 5:8 says: *Be alert and of sober mind. Your enemy the devil prowls around like a roaring lion looking for someone to devour.* He's not going to quit. He's pacing, day by day, hour by hour, looking for a crack or a weak spot where he can wage war—even if it's temporarily. He's seeking whom he can devour, whom he can sift as wheat, slowly but surely. But when you live with The Advantage, when you live with Holy Spirit as your guide, your peace and your comfort, as the verse says, *a stranger you will not follow*.

1 Kings 19:11-12 says: *The Lord said, "Go out and stand on the mountain in the presence of the Lord, for the Lord is about to pass by." Then a great and powerful wind tore the mountains apart and shattered the rocks before the Lord, but the Lord was not in the wind. After the wind there was an earthquake, but the Lord was not in the earthquake. After the earthquake came a fire, but the Lord was not in the fire and after the fire came a gentle whisper.*

The Lord wasn't in the wind. He wasn't in the earthquake. He wasn't even in the fire. So many times, we look for God to move in a big, loud, rambunctious way. We look for the fireworks on top of the hill, the flashing lights and the loud boom. We look for him to move mountains right before our very eyes—when He's clearly instructed us to speak to the mountain and it will move. But, as the passage above reflects, the Lord spoke in a gentle whisper. He didn't scream and shout. He didn't holler at the top of His lungs. He spoke in a small, calm whisper. Any time someone speaks in a whisper, one has to listen intently and carefully. If there's any surrounding noise or interference, one must shut it down to hear the voice of the whisperer.

Likewise, we have to turn down the noise of our lives. We have to minimize distractions. We have to be intentional about spending time with Holy Spirit and reading God's Word. Don't start your day without communing with Holy Spirit. He's your guide, your GPS—not just for the large things and the big decisions, but the small ones, too. He wants to be involved in every decision of your day-to-day life, walking with you hand in hand, step by step the whole way. This is the advantage of living and walking daily with Holy Spirit. When you set time aside for Him, listen intently for His voice, and commune with Him regularly, you won't ever be lost; you won't ever "not" know which direction to turn. But in order to hear that still small voice, you'll have to silence the noise and center yourself to hear clear instructions. This is The Advantage!

Be mindful of who the voice will come through. It may not always be in your place of worship. It may not always be in your sacred place of prayer or through another Christian. It may not come through someone in the five-fold ministry. His voice is everywhere. Pay attention to small details, nuances, shifts, and the movement of the wind. Sometimes, it will be in the beauty shop or the barber shop. It may be something you read on a billboard. It could even be somewhere that you least expect in a tragedy or a moment of confusion. It could be an Asian or a Muslim. It could be a Jew or a Catholic. It could be an adult, or even yes, a child. His voice is everywhere. Don't be limited to the noise of the familiar of religion. Don't expect the voice of Holy Spirit to always be where you found it the last time. God has people everywhere and His voice can come through any person—including those who are not born again.

Holy Spirit can drop a word in the mouth of an unbeliever that speaks directly to you. Don't limit Holy Spirit. Don't limit His ways, His movements, His motions, and His personality to just what you know. Remember, Holy Spirit superintends the affairs of men—government, kingdoms and hierarchies. There is no space in this universe Holy Spirit doesn't occupy. When you look for the whisper, you must be open to the many ways and diverse opportunities He will seize to speak to you. In that tragedy, He's speaking. In that mistake, He's speaking. In that missed opportunity, He's speaking. In life and in death, He's speaking and when you're up and when you're low, Holy Spirit is speaking. Don't let the external circumstance prevent you from leaning in to see what He will say. He that hath an ear, let him hear what the spirit is saying to the church.

The church is not just a building. The church is a people. There are people everywhere Holy Spirit is using in this hour to speak to you. Don't let your own prejudice drown out His voice. Don't let your own bias drown out His voice. Don't let your own fear drown out His voice. Don't allow regret, doubt and doctrine make you deaf to Holy Spirit's voice. Blessed is he, which is happy, fortunate and highly favored. Blessed is he that can hear. If you can hear Holy Spirit's voice before you make a decision, you will save yourself time and money. Consult with Holy Spirit. Ask Him questions about your plan and the direction you desire.

The navigational system doesn't automatically direct you. You must input information. You know where you want to go. You just don't know how to get there. You put in the address of the desired location at which you want to arrive. From this moment forward, do the exact same thing with Holy Spirit. Take the time to input the information in His care. Where do you desire to go? What do you desire to do? He will lay out the map and the plan step by step for you to arrive safely to your desired destination. Don't be taken aback if He alters your route. Don't argue with Him because you think you already know. Allow Him to navigate your course. He gives you the competitive edge in every situation. If you don't hear the first time, there is a built-in recalculation in Holy Spirit. If you missed it the first time, He always gives you another chance. You still must hear His voice. The voice of Holy Spirit is intended to correct your course. If you fail to hear, you will continue to make the same mistakes that will keep you in the position of lack, misery, pain and suffering. It's not always somebody else that needs to change. That's what the noise tells you. The noise says, "It's somebody else's fault." The noise will make you a victim. The noise will tell you you're at a disadvantage. But when you can silence the noise and hear the course correction that comes from Holy Spirit, you will truly live life with an advantage.

Delete excessive noise that blocks Holy Spirit's voice.

Life with "The Advantage"

John 14:16-17 *And I will pray the Father, and He will give you another Helper, that He may abide with you forever—the Spirit of truth, whom the world cannot receive, because it neither sees Him nor knows Him; but you know Him, for He dwells with you and will be in you.*

John 16:7 *Nevertheless I tell you the truth. It is to your advantage that I go away; for if I do not go away, the Helper will not come to you; but if I depart, I will send Him to you.*

I am persuaded that approximately 70-75% of the Christian population does *not* know Holy Spirit intimately. They have heard about Him. They have attached Him to the end of prayers. They make Him a template for baptisms, weddings and other sacred services. But to have an intimate walk, relationship and fellowship with Holy Spirit, in the same fashion we have pursued Jesus Christ, we have to pursue Holy Spirit. Jesus Christ has come to save us from our sins. He is our Savior. He now is our Lord because of His resurrection power. But to live this life with Jesus alone puts you at a severe *disadvantage*.

The popular song, *A Little More Jesus*, disturbs me. I understand that we live in a season of pop culture where we have to meet people where they are. Do we realize that the lyrics to the song are absolute errors based on Scripture? As Believers, there is no more Jesus that He can give us. He is now seated at the right hand of the Father. He is making intercession for us. So, there is no more Jesus that can be given to you to help you along your way. But the passages from the Word of God above let us know that Jesus left us in good hands. He knew we would need help. He knew we would need comfort. He knew we would sometimes feel like an orphan. He knew the people of God would feel neglected because He had to go away. The people of God would no longer have Jesus in the physical presence anymore. But there was a promise from the Father given that after Jesus accomplished His assignment, the Advantage would come. And that promise, could not take place unless Jesus went away.

So, it was to our advantage that He went away. Had He stayed, the people of God would never know the Spirit of Truth. They would never have the guide or the power. He was only here as our Savior. Once He went to the cross, shed His blood and reconciled us back to God, His assignment was finished. But He didn't leave us alone, without a comforter or guide. He left us with Holy Ghost. Although the world is not able to physically see Him, He dwells in us.

Acts 1:8 says: *But ye shall receive power, after that the Holy Ghost is come upon you: and ye shall be witnesses unto me both in Jerusalem, and in all Judaea, and in Samaria, and unto the uttermost part of the earth.* On the day of Pentecost, Holy Ghost fell upon all who were gathered in the room together. There is a great benefit of having Holy Spirit living in you. Many times, we overlook Holy Spirit *in* us so that we can get to the experience of the Holy Spirit coming *upon* us. When Holy Spirit comes upon us, we get all the bells and whistles—the gifts, the power, the authority, the supernatural edge. But Holy Spirit is not just *upon* you in Pentecost; He's *in* you. We have to learn to embrace the true person of Holy Spirit. He is not a mystical dove. He is not smoke. He is not a mirror. He is a Person. He is not the junior part of the God-head. He is God. He is equal to the Father and equal to the Son; co-equal, and co-essential.

Without Holy Spirit, we would not have the Bible. It is Holy Spirit that moved on the people to write as it quickened them. Without Holy Spirit, we would not have Jesus because it was Holy Spirit that overshadowed Mary when she conceived. Without Holy Spirit, there would be no resurrection. Jesus, who had raised others, could not raise himself. So, the Father sent the Holy Ghost to raise Jesus from the dead. Holy Spirit is not an inanimate object or something that floats. It is not an invisible ghost. If you've ever heard of the Trinity, that they are three in one, that theory is incorrect. They are not three in one, they are ONE in THREE. THEY are three distinct Persons. As the Son was an individual distinct from the Father, so is Holy Spirit an individual distinct from the Son. Neither of them is less than the other.

- **THEY are absolute omniscient.**
- **THEY are absolute omnipresent.**

- ❖ **THEY are absolute omnipotent.**
- ❖ **THEY operate in three distinct dispensations, with diverse applications and methods.**
- ❖ **THEY are *never* divided.**
- ❖ **THEY *never* have conflict.**
- ❖ **THEY *never* rival each other.**
- ❖ **THEY don't compete with one another.**

If you honor Holy Spirit, Jesus does not get jealous. There is no competition between Jesus, Father and Holy Spirit. Jesus said Holy Spirit will come and glorify Him. Jesus then glorifies the Father. There is absolutely no division between the Father, the Word and the Spirit. These three are one and they *always* agree. In the first dispensation, "Day One," the Father spoke and said, *"Let there be...."* The Word then came forth and the Spirit activated and brought manifestation.

- ❖ **THEY operate as one.**

In the second dispensation, "Day Two," the Father cried out, realizing He needed someone to go to reconcile man back to Him, the virgin named Mary was impregnated with Jesus by Holy Spirit. At the time, Mary was engaged to a righteous man named Joseph. It wasn't enough that she was a virgin; but that she was engaged to a righteous man. There were more than 8,000 virgins at this time, but the parents who would raise this child had to be *righteous*. Mary conceived Jesus and raised Him as a human with a Divine purpose. Living with Joseph as a child and growing up under the authority of his parents, learning the trade of His earthly father, Joseph, Jesus had a semi-normal life; but at the age of 30, He appeared at the River Jordan to be baptized and to fulfill His Heavenly Father's original intent for Him. **Matthew 3:15** says: *And Jesus answering said unto him, "Suffer it to be so now: for thus it becomes us to fulfill all righteousness." Then he suffered him.*

At that moment, Holy Spirit came and anointed Jesus so that He could do good and deliver those who are bound by demons. Jesus could not operate minus Holy Ghost. He could not operate minus the Father. The Father could not operate minus the Son, nor Holy Spirit. But it is in **John 14** that Jesus explains to the disciples that it was for their *advantage* that He go. Although He was no longer *with* them, He assured them that the Holy Ghost was *in* them and would guide them from that point on.

Holy Spirit will guide you. He will speak truth to you. He will be in you to help you with the things that baffle you, the things you've worked on and seen no success, and the things that you don't know. He will be in you. He will impregnate your spirit with spiritual DNA so that you will never be alone again. *You'll never be confused again.* He is your true Advantage, given to you as the leverage you need to live above mediocrity and failure. This is better than the days when Jesus walked the earth. This is better than when the disciples and people of God watched Jesus work. The day we live in now is a better day.

John 16:8 says: *And when He has come, He will convict the world of sin, and of righteousness, and of judgment.* **John 16:12-13** *"I still have many things to say to you, but you cannot bear them now. However, when He, the Spirit of truth, has come, He will guide you into all truth; for He will not speak on His own authority, but whatever He hears He will speak; and He will tell you things to come."*

Imagine what your life looks like if, and when, you have all truth living on the inside of you. Imagine the *advantage* that you have over people who are not believers. You have an advantage over your circumstances. You have an advantage over every situation. The Spirit of Truth, Holy Spirit, lives inside of you and prompts you, nudges you, guides you and directs you through your human spirit. You are *not* without answers. You are *not* called to be confused. You have all truth because the Spirit of Truth lives inside you. You are not just saved; you are wise. You have discernment. You will even know things before they happen. Holy Spirit is not here to make you dance and feel good. He is here to give you truth in every area of your life. He is the genius mind of God, and He gives you genius ideas, plans, visions, purpose, directives, instructions, secrets, unfolds mysteries, guides you around trouble, takes you over your liabilities and human weakness, informs you, conforms you, transforms you and ultimately becomes your very best friend and confidant in life. What a GIFT! What an ADVANTAGE Holy Spirit is in our lives.

Holy Spirit has in Him every minute thought of the Father. Jesus does *not* know the mind of the Father. Holy Spirit is the only one who intimately knows the mind of the Father. No man can know the mind of a man, but he can know the spirit of that man. For example, you can sleep in the same bed with someone and not know what's on their mind. You can eat at the same table with your spouse and your children and not have a clue what's on their minds. We, as people, are so compartmentalized that we can function without anyone ever guessing what's on our minds. But our spirit knows what's on our minds. It is the same with Holy Spirit, He knows the mind of the Father at all times.

In **1 Corinthians 2**, Paul tells us that the only person who knows the mind of God is the Holy Spirit. The same Holy Spirit who knows the mind of God lives in you. There is no reason you should be confused. You shouldn't be overwhelmed, frustrated and baffled. The challenge is not whether or not the Holy Spirit lives in you—it does. The challenge is that you have not cultivated a relationship with Him. The Holy Spirit won't share secrets with someone who does not have a relationship with Him. But it is the Father's good pleasure to give you the secrets and the keys to every locked door in your life. But you must develop a relationship with He who knows all. You don't have to tear up your life or relationships and spend another 15 years trying to fix it. If you develop a relationship with the Holy Spirit, every situation will turn out to be truth and good.

God doesn't want you to trust your wisdom. Holy Spirit won't let you argue. He won't let you curse. He won't let you act a fool in public. Holy Spirit will tell you to walk away. Once you develop a relationship and know His voice, and know how He operates, you won't have to repent for something the Holy Ghost has already helped you prevent and avoid.

In **1 Corinthians 1:5** Paul says: *And I, brethren, when I came to you, did not come with excellence of speech or of wisdom declaring to you the testimony of God. For I determined not to know anything among you except Jesus Christ and Him crucified. I was with you in weakness, in fear, and in much trembling. And my speech and my preaching were not with persuasive words of human wisdom, but in demonstration of the Spirit and of power, that your faith should not be in the wisdom of men but in the power of God.*

Your wisdom is an offense to Holy Spirit. There is nothing in your carnal mind that is pleasing to God. The fleshly mind is hostile to God. Whenever you choose to use your wisdom over the wisdom of Holy Spirit, you will have calamity. Your wisdom is smart and logical; however, it is limited, *very* limited. It is not spiritual, and it is not connected to the mind of God. When we rely on our own intelligence, we make a mess. God set it up like this so when things work out, you'll know it didn't happen because of the wisdom of man, but because of the power of God. No one is more deserving of the glory. But there is also no one more desiring of the glory than God. He not only deserves it; He desires it. He wants the glory for turning that situation around. When you rely on your wisdom, He is offended because you didn't give Him the opportunity to fix it so He can get the glory and honor Jesus.

Holy Spirit is smarter than any textbook. He's smarter than the Bible. Holy Spirit moved upon men and women to write the Bible. Without the guidance of Holy Spirit, the people would not have been able to successfully write it. While He may have shared a great amount of His knowledge and wisdom in the Bible, that doesn't mean He doesn't have more information to share. 1 **Corinthians 2:9**: *Eye hath not seen, nor ear heard, neither have entered into the heart of man, the things which God hath prepared for them that love him.* That means He has much more in store than what we see written. While it's great to gather knowledge, if it doesn't come from Holy Spirit, it won't give you the results God intended you to have. It won't give you *The Advantage. By keeping you in the truth at ALL times in all things; Holy Spirit will keep you out of error.*

If you are baffled and confused, it is because you are not engaging the Spirit of Truth. You do not fellowship with Him. You are not nurturing the relationship. You do not engage Him in your affairs. The operating system of God resides in you. You cannot live your life on software alone. But the operating system is the DNA of God and all that He knows is inside of you. You have *The*

Advantage. He knows where all the money is, so you shouldn't be broke. You shouldn't have any lack. He knows creativity because He created the heavens and the earth. So, there isn't anything that He *can't* create. So, if you need a job or a new opportunity, you need to engage the Spirit of Truth that lives on the inside of you. Talk to Him and allow Him to start talking to you so that He can guide you to where the money, the wealth and the resources lie. He knows where the opportunity and the favor are; He knows how to get you behind the door. He knows how to put your name in their mind.

Imagine how we look to the Father when we live at such a level of disadvantage, even though we have been given *The Advantage.* He is not a mystic. He is not a strong wind that blows. He is a Person. He wants you to know Him and be in relationship with Him. He wants you to ask Him questions. He wants you to seek Him for guidance. When you first open your eyes in the morning, greet and acknowledge Him. When you get up in the morning, you should speak to Him, "Good Morning, Holy Spirit." After all, He kept you through the night. He brought you to the morning light. He kept the robbers out. The alarm clock didn't wake you up this morning. He did. He kept your heart beating. The very least you could do is thank Him and acknowledge Him.

So many people want the *Upper Room* experience. They want to be endued with power. They want to be able to wrestle an elephant and pull down strongholds in the spirit realm. They want to speak in tongues. Some even want their ministry to be powerful. But after you can get all of that, which is the *"upon" Upper Room* experience, you've got to be able to handle the *within* experience of intimacy. You must pursue life with Holy Spirit. There must be an intimate relationship after the power of Pentecost engulfs your life, a relationship before ministry; a relationship before miracles and the supernatural exploits promised by Father God. There is a life with Holy Spirit that produces a wonderful ongoing intimate relationship. He will entrust everything He knows and has to those that will live with Him intimately.

Not only do you have to talk to Him, but you have to listen to Him. You have to let Him guide you. Allow Him to take over in a situation. When He says speak, speak. When He says be quiet, be quiet. Holy Spirit leaves an imprint on our spirit with the nature of God. Holy Spirit does not live in your heart or emotions. He does not live in your soul. He lives in your spirit. Even after the imprint, your soul still needs to be converted. Your mind still needs to be renewed. But your spirit man has the DNA of God. You are now a participant of the divine nature. You have escaped the corruption of the world. While other people fall to the lust of the flesh or the eye, you, as a believer have the nature of God in your spirit. You have the advantage over the lust of the eye, the lust of your flesh, the pride of life. You are no longer a victim. But you have to listen to His voice. You have to take heed to His nudging. To some, He speaks audibly. To others, He speaks visually. You have to pay attention to Him. You have to become familiar with the way in which He speaks directly to you. It's not nausea. It's not butterflies in your stomach. Have you ever heard someone say, "Something told me not to…?" It wasn't *something*. It's Holy Ghost that lives on the inside of you! Don't disregard Holy Ghost. It warns you and guides you. Pay attention to the God in you!

The only thing that you now have to wrestle with is your carnal mind. Your mind operates against Holy Ghost. Your fleshly mind, which is personality and your temperament, is constantly at war with Holy Ghost. Your mind is used to calling the shots. It's used to directing you, and most of our lives, we live by our soul, our emotions and our will. The carnal mind hates the fact that you now have Holy Spirit dwelling on the inside of you. The intent and the ultimate purpose of Holy Spirit is to present you faultless at the end of your life. Every day, Holy Spirit changes you, little by little. He's rearranging things in you. He comes into you as you are, but He won't leave you as you are. His assignment is to transform you into the image of God's Son. People want to be able to shout and cast out devils, but you won't listen when He tells you not to go that way. You don't want to listen when He tells you not to wear that. You want to be a wonder behind the pulpit, but you won't pay attention to Him when He tells you to put the credit card up and get out of that store. If He can't trust you to be quiet or speak when He tells you to, why would He trust you with a microphone? Why would He trust you with a church? Why would He trust you with millions when you can't tell where the hundreds went that He gave you?

Some people are comfortable living in lack. It's the norm for them. They don't expect to see any growth or manifestation of anything different than what they've always received. Most times, lack is a direct result of a personal decision. While we deal with things on the surface, Holy Ghost searches the deep things of God. Ask the Holy Spirit what you should do and how you should handle day-to-day matters. Ask Him to bring you the mind of the Father on your matters.

One year, I was on a cruise with my husband in Belize. We paid for a scuba diving excursion, but once I got there, I didn't want to get off the boat. The person in charge realized my fear and asked me if I would like to get in the water. Now, when I paid the $100, I thought I wanted to get in the water. But once I got out there, I wasn't sure. He took a rope out of a container and tied one end to me and the other end to my husband. He told me that since my husband knew how to swim, all I had to do was keep my head down and look around. I didn't have to kick or swim. Yet, I was terrified. Even once I got into the water, I kept popping my head up—until the instructor told me if I didn't stop doing that, I would drown my husband. I had to trust the rope. In order to see the phenomenal things that exist underwater, I had to trust the rope. Suddenly, I felt the peace of God. Once I opened my eyes, I could see the beauty that existed underwater. At some point, I was so captivated by the things we saw, I didn't realize how deep out into the water we were. Since I live on top of the earth, I didn't realize this world exists underwater. There was a totally different dimension—just like Holy Spirit wants to show us. He wants to show us great and mighty things. But because we won't trust the rope, we never get to see the deep!

This is your advantage. You should not live a life of fear, lack and challenge. If the same Holy Spirit that raised Jesus from the dead lives in you, won't He heal your body from sickness and disease? Will He not walk with you through your day-to-day challenges? Will He not make sure that every need is met and then some? There is no greater power. You don't need to seek psychics to guide your life. Don't seek the soothsayers to guide your life. Don't gamble with your life. The mysteries you have not solved. The small answers you don't have yet. The things that remain hidden from you—they can all be obtained through Holy Spirit that lives in you to bring you all truth.

You have an advantage over your weaknesses. You have an advantage over your parents' DNA. No one can curse you. When the Holy Spirit lives on the inside of you, it is impossible for you to be under a spell of any demonic force. It's a great experience to speak in tongues and have a great ministry, but that's a third-day experience. But with a second-day experience came the impartation of Holy Ghost. Without Holy Ghost, people can drink anything, they can go anywhere, and they can wear anything—without any form of conviction. Some people can curse someone out and it doesn't bother them. That is proof that there is no Holy Ghost dwelling on the inside of them. It is Holy Ghost that constrains you. It dresses you. It stops you from drinking. It stops you from cursing people out. It stops you from fornicating. You are too old, and you've walked with Christ for too long, to still sleep around! Once you have the indwelling of Holy Ghost, you can't just do what you want to do and say what you want to say.

Romans 8:2 says, *For the law of the Spirit of life in Christ Jesus has made me free from the law of sin and death.* It's important to understand, however, that you won't be delivered from *everything*. But Holy Spirit will give you the advantage over it. God knows that I love a man. It doesn't matter if it's a white man, black man, African man or an Arab man. If God made anything better than a man, He kept it for Himself. But God knew it would have taken Him too long to deliver me from desire for man. But Holy Ghost gives me the advantage over those desires. It's still there. He has not delivered me from that desire. But I have the *advantage* over that thing. Because that is my appetite, He had to put something in me to have an advantage over it. Some people like weed. Some people like crack. Maybe your desire is Hennessy. Everyone has something they like that God will not deliver them from—but He gave you the advantage over it.

If the Spirit of God dwells within you, and you cultivate the relationship with Him, that influence in your life will be more powerful than your very own flesh. God doesn't have to take every bad thing out of you. Many times, so we understand His Grace is sufficient. But you have a power that guides you over the things that are left. You have power that guides you under it. It guides you around it. But you must have a relationship. Invite Him into your life. Invite Him into your day. Ask Holy Spirit to command your day. It is the power to help you overcome your past hurts and past fears. It is the power that helps you overcome your environment, your childhood, and your mindsets. It helps you overcome the viruses, the bugs, the Trojan horses. You may have had some bad memories and some bad encounters, but there is a power that lives within you when you're not in church and the musician is not around. When your back is up against the wall and you can hear your own mind giving you bad advice, Holy Ghost takes over because it lives in you!

There are people who will shout in church, but don't have any victory. They run laps around the pulpit, but still maintain their bad attitude. They still play the organ, but they have a horrible temper. They teach Sunday school classes and direct the choir, but still don't have The Advantage. It was for our advantage that Jesus went away, and Holy Spirit has come. Jesus put a resident helper in us before He went away. The physical person, Jesus Christ, is powerless to operate in the earthly realm today. His mission is finished and complete. But Holy Ghost lives in you. Why would you talk to someone who lives a long distance, when you've got somebody living in you? If someone is in another country, why would you talk to them, when you could talk to somebody who lives in your house and doesn't have to spend money?

When you walk, He walks in you. When people curse you out on your job, He is with you. Ask Him what to do. When your bills come up short, sit down and talk to Him. Get to know Him. Get to know how He moves and ways He wants you to go. Spend some time with Him and you'll learn His voice. If you're looking for a mate, you need to talk to Holy Spirit. If your child needs a scholarship, take it up with Holy Spirit. The mate or the money is not going to fall from Heaven. You have to talk to the Helper. He'll tell you what to do. He'll give you Grace. He'll give you wisdom and favor. He'll give you *The Advantage*!

When you accepted Christ as your Lord and Savior, Holy Spirit sealed you. You may know Him when He moves mightily in a service. You may know Him when you see people get healed and delivered. But do you know Him *in* you? He is a great friend and companion. He wants you to have a relationship with Him. Don't ignore Him and treat Him as if He doesn't even exist. He'll give you truth in all situations. You don't have to live in stress and anxiety. Unlock the treasure that Jesus has put on the inside of you.

I don't know when I stopped participating in fleshly things. I don't know when I stopped smoking cigarettes, and I don't know the exact day I stopped engaging in sin. I didn't have to grit my teeth. I didn't have to work at it. I didn't have to use will power. I engaged Holy Spirit, my Advantage. I just decided one day I wanted life with Him.

I didn't go through a 12-step program, but when I talked to Holy Spirit, my entire life changed. Talk to Holy Spirit every day and when He gives you directions, follow them. It makes no sense to have the advantage and not *live with the advantage on a daily basis in everything.*

Life with Him on a daily basis is a much richer experience than life without Him.

The Seal

Our primary purpose in this life is to be filled with all of the fullness of God. Everything else is secondary. We are to pursue the length, the depth and the height of the fullness of God. It is important to understand, by the blood of Jesus Christ, we have been adopted and accepted in Christ. There is nothing else we have to do to be accepted. We don't have to do any more work. Jesus paid it all. **Ephesians 1:13-14** says: *In whom ye also trusted, after that ye heard the word of truth, the gospel of your salvation: in whom also after that ye believed, ye were sealed with that Holy Spirit of promise, Which is the earnest of our inheritance until the redemption of the purchased possession, unto the praise of His glory.* We have been sealed through Holy Ghost.

When I think of the seal, I think of the notary. That is a legally binding seal that can never be undone and whenever the notary stamps it with the seal of approval, that's it. It is now a legally binding document. Likewise, we are sealed, and the Holy Ghost is the notary. We have been sealed with Holy Spirit of promise who is the guarantee of our inheritance. No matter how crazy we may act along the way that notary seal is still on our lives. He knows those that belong to Him. There is a day coming where He will redeem you back to Himself and not hold your sins against you. This rich salvation is nothing that man could have thought of. This is authentic. When I believed the gospel and I received Christ, at that moment that I believed, I was sealed.

When my mother made preserves, she put them into Mason jars. While we wanted some of the preserves right then and there, my mother knew they had to be sealed. So, she put the preserves into the jars and put the seal on so tight, that when the time came to take the lid off, you had to pry it off. But whether it was months or years later, everything that was in that jar was just as fresh as the moment my mother had put the preserves in the jar. When Jesus comes back to redeem us, and He breaks the Seal, we will be just as if we have never sinned. He knows those that bear His own Seal. It's a Seal of the King. Our salvation is sealed until He comes back to break it.

Anything that happened once the seal was applied never affected the contents. It may have disturbed the outer container, but it never disturbed the treasure inside. The spirit man does not sin. The body and the soul may commit sin, but the Seal is on the spirit man. The Seal doesn't allow the sin to seep into the spirit. So, I can be in the club, with a drink in my hand, and the wrong man by my side, and start singing a gospel song. I may have meant to sing another song, but my spirit man allowed a gospel song to come out. There is more gospel sung in the clubs than what people know. When a Christian gets drunk, they always go back to church in their minds. They are simply sealed Christians misbehaving. But the Seal is not removed. God won't let us break the Seal. You have a guarantee that you are sealed.

It's not just good enough to know you are saved. You need to know why and what happened to produce the authentic Jesus Christ in you. Rehearse it. We are now partakers. We are fellow heirs of the same body of the promise of Christ through the gospel. Authenticity deals with intent. If you have something authentic, you have to know the original intent of the creator from the beginning. Because we are now the body of Christ, we can now finally get back to the original intent of God's purpose and plan. The original intent is through the church of the authentic Christ; we will teach to principalities and powers the manifold wisdom of God. We will teach demons. We will teach principalities. We will teach them the wisdom of the riches of God.

Many of us practice salvation but don't have a clue as to how we really got saved. We don't know what it really cost Jesus for us to be saved. We don't know how to fully make our salvation experience authentic. We just know that we gave our life to Jesus Christ. We have to learn what it truly cost Jesus for us to be authentic. We have to understand the price that was paid. We must understand the Seal, and the purpose of the Seal. We are the brand of God. We carry His insignia on our spirit. We are branded with His Seal, His initials, His signature, His DNA. His character comes within us the moment we believe the gospel. The Seal is unbreakable, impenetrable and defies compromise by outside elements of darkness and dubious intent.

The dictionary defines the *seal* as, *"a device or substance that is used to join two things together so as to prevent them from coming apart or to prevent anything from passing between them; something that secures (such as a wax seal on a document); a closure that must be broken to be opened and thus reveals tampering."* God loves us enough to put on us the Seal that keeps us from being tampered with. Isn't this an *advantage*? The advantage of having the Seal on our lives is that we have a confidence in our secured relationship with God, while others walk in fear of losing a relationship with their god. As believers of Jesus Christ, we have an advantage over other religious followers. They have no seal, no security and no confidence in the permanence of their relationship. With our Seal of Holy Spirit, He is the guarantor. He is the cosigner. He is the one with good credit. He secures our connectivity to God, until we are redeemed from our bodies in this earthly journey. We have no worry about losing God or God losing us. God cannot lose us or disown us. He cannot act as if we don't belong to Him. He will never forsake us. He will never abandon us, because He knows His own. How does He know us? He knows us by the Seal. His stamp, His brand rests on us.

In business, the identity of any manufacturer or business name is called their *brand*. A brand is what separates you from other commodities that may claim to do the same thing. How do you know the distinction between laundry detergent and automobiles? How do you recognize the uniqueness between manufacturers of clothing from another? Are all clothes the same quality? Do they all do the same thing? Are some better than others? So, in the vast world of choices, most of us stick to and have a preference for a certain brand. Some of us choose based on childhood preferences. Our parents used a certain brand of soap or cleanser. We could walk in the house and smell certain cleansers. We know by that smell our parents were cleaning the house. Most times, the products used in our childhood are what we use as adults. It's called *brand loyalty*.

We didn't know we were being branded. As we became adults, we went directly to the aisle and selected the same products our parents used. But because of childhood relationships, we were captured and most times, have remained loyal to a certain brand. Commercials flood our airways. They compare one brand to another. And we have myriads of options now in a vast world of marketing and business. Yet, we go back to what we know and are familiar with. It doesn't matter what new product comes out. We may try it for a minute, but eventually we shake our heads and go back to the brand we know. Whether we know it or not, these experiences and exposures have put a seal on us emotionally. So, we feel almost disloyal when we choose something different over the brand we are familiar with.

The Seal of God is just like this. It operates identically. We are sealed. We prefer our brand over others. We may investigate other options, but the Seal has gripped us. Emotionally, the Seal has created a loyalty for our brand. Even when we wander off, we come back to our brand because it's what we know. It's not us that does it, it's the Seal. The Advantage, the Seal keeps us, holds us, grips us and sustains us. Even though we are not always loyal, and can be found in seasons of offense and disappointment, the Seal prevents tampering. We have now been brought together as one with Christ. The relationship is secure. We ourselves cannot break the Seal. The application of the Seal, the strength of the Seal, is immutable. Not even you, reading this book right now, can break the Seal. If you lie dormant for years, if you don't pick up your Bible, if you don't attend church, if you don't pray—the Seal is still there. The Seal is still there doing its job. Although Holy Spirit will not push you back into an active relationship, *The Advantage* is that it prevents another relationship from being engaged. You still can't go anywhere. You cannot become an active Muslim or atheist. You can't become something else. You may not be active; however, Holy Spirit prevents other opportunities from breaking the Seal.

At the right time, something will prick your heart again. Something will turn your mind back to church, back to praying, back to reading the Bible. It could be a tragedy, trauma, sickness, financial crisis—that suddenly strikes you and alters your life. You think, "I need to go to church." But who gave you that thought? You cry out, "Oh God! Help me!" Who gave you that prayer when you haven't prayed for years? You haven't picked up a Bible in years. But all of a sudden, you cry out for God because the Seal was never broken. You don't have to go searching for where to get help. You still have *The Advantage*, you still have Holy Spirit, and He will put in your mind, at the right time, the right thought and direction you need in order to return to an active relationship with Father God.

The Seal is never broken! What an Advantage!

Dimensions

We learn in **Ephesians 3:10** the original intent of God: *To the intent that now unto the principalities and powers in heavenly places might be known by the church the manifold wisdom of God.* It was God's intent, through the church; His manifold wisdom would be made known to principalities. That is a powerful statement.

In the Greek, to operate in the fullness of God is explained in another way. It means you may be fully able to go further and to know the full dimensions of the spiritual purpose of Christ. You will be full to capacity. The breadth implies that the reach of the church will be worldwide. It takes me 18 hours to get to Australia. The same Bible, the same Jesus and the same Holy Spirit reside even down under. When I speak in Australia, and I tell them to turn to Ephesians, they open their Bibles to Ephesians. When I went to Ireland, in the basement of a newspaper factory, they had to blindfold me to go in because of the war. They weren't allowed to have Bibles, but they had hymnals. They sang the same hymns that we sing in America. They sang it the same way with the same words. That's the breadth of God. When I went to another part of the world, there were no televisions, no cable and no satellite. But they could quote Scriptures. I was in awe at how the gospel of Jesus Christ makes it to even the lowest part of the globe, and even beyond that. They didn't have clothes, and they didn't have running water. But they could quote **Psalm 91,** just like I did. They knew the story of Joshua and Jericho. They knew the story of Jonah in the whale. This doesn't happen without the church teaching the manifold wisdom of God!

You cannot stop the gospel. It will get to wherever God intends for it to go. But if you don't understand what you are a part of, it will never be authentic to you. The breadth of God is not just for our time period. It will be extended through all ages. Your grandmother might have known the Lord. Your great grandmother may have known the Lord. The length after we are gone will extend long after us. That which is authentic has length, width and breadth. When Peter preached on the day of Pentecost, he preached that it wasn't just for us. It is for our children and our children's children. It is for them that are far off. The unsearchable riches are of God and represent the depth. It doesn't matter if I die. If it's authentic, it will go past my death.

The depth of it is the profound wisdom of God that no creature can fathom. The height is beyond the reach of any enemy that will try to deprive us of it. The height is the realm of principalities and spiritual wickedness. Spiritual wickedness exists in high places. But the height of the love of God far surpasses any interference from any spiritual wickedness or power. God's original intent was to establish a place for us in Him that no one can take away. Because of the width, the length, the depth and the height, no witch or warlock can destroy us.

God's plan is that we are filled with all of that—the length, the width, the depth and the height. Everything else is secondary. If the entire length, depth, width and height of God are in you, where is there room for anything else? Authenticity is not filling up the pews and searching for greater ministries. It's not about being famous from the pulpit. Just because a nurse can give a shot doesn't mean she understands the body and how it works. If she gives the shot in the wrong spot, a person can be paralyzed immediately. When people are in charge of the church, and they don't have the correct information, they have to adapt the church to their ignorance. The body of Christ becomes paralyzed. Their leaders adapt to their ignorance. When you don't understand the authenticity of what you are now a part of, one must adapt according to their ignorance. This is how the church lost its authenticity. Ungodly men came into the church, and became like clouds with no water.

Holy Spirit desires we understand the dimensions that are available in the relationship with him. I want to explain what the dimensions are, how vital they each are to your life. By explaining them in detail, you can assess yourself and your capacity for Holy Spirit. You may discover that you have mastered one dimension, or even two. But if we do not have the fullness of Holy Spirit, we still have time to make up the shortage once we understand the various dimensions. This helps us evaluate our relationship with Holy Spirit.

❖ **Width is defined as the largeness of extent or scope.**

❖ **Length is defined as the longer or longest dimension of an object.**

❖ **Depth is defined as the degree of intensity; the quality or state of being complete or thorough.**

❖ **Height is defined as the most advanced or extreme point of something.**

Ezekiel 47:1-5 says: *Afterward he brought me again unto the door of the house; and, behold, waters issued out from under the threshold of the house eastward: for the forefront of the house stood toward the east, and the waters came down from under from the right side of the house, at the south side of the altar. Then brought he me out of the way of the gate northward, and led me about the way without unto the utter gate by the way that looketh eastward; and, behold, there ran out waters on the right side. And when the man that had the line in his hand went forth eastward, he measured a thousand cubits, and he brought me through the waters; the waters were to the **ankles**. Again he measured a thousand, and brought me through the waters; the waters were to the **knees**. Again he measured a thousand, and brought me through; the waters were to the **loins**. Afterward he measured a thousand; and it was a river that I could not pass over: for the **waters***

were risen, waters to swim in, a river that could not be passed over.

❖ **Ankles: the slender part of the leg above the foot.**

❖ **Knees: the central area of the leg between the thigh and the lower leg.**

❖ **Loins: the parts of the body between the hips and the lower ribs, especially regarded as the seat of physical strength and generative power.**

❖ **Overflow: to be filled or supplied with great measure.**

Now, let's deal with this. In each of these scriptures, we learn that capacities of Holy Spirit vary and each of us must pursue and apprehend the dimensions that are available. Oftentimes, we settle for the dimension we are most familiar with, not knowing or being ignorant of the fullness that is available to every believer. We suffer greatly when we fail to be full, when we fail to pursue, when we fail to be aware of, to be knowledgeable of the multiple facets, nuances and capacities of Holy Spirit. This is a lifelong pursuit, and it must be a priority in your life. To know Holy Spirit on every dimension—not just one or two—but all that is available.

Let's deal with the width. The width of Holy Spirit, in order with Scripture, is the first dimension. It is the first mentioned by the apostle Paul and lays the groundwork for your growth and development. But it is not the only dimension Holy Spirit wants to give of Himself. The apostle Paul says, in **Ephesians 3:16** that he would grant you according to the riches of His glory, to be strengthened with might through His spirit in the inner man. Do you hear what he is saying? The riches of His glory-that your inner man, through Holy Spirit, would be strong and powerful. But if you fail to pursue the riches, you will not have all that the Father wants you to have and experience. I believe the majority of the church is here. They have the width. This is a legitimate dimension that is not to be taken lightly. Holy Spirit is present, but only in one dimension. I don't believe the church is impotent. I don't believe the church is powerless. I don't believe the church of Jesus Christ is lacking. But I do believe our capacity is too small. I do believe there is a lack of teaching and understanding and the first measure is not enough. This is why we must go to the next dimension and teach people to have a thirst, a personal thirst, for all that is available. Too many times, our parishioners are limited based on what they have been taught—or what they are not being taught. But there has to be something inside of them, individually, that says, "I want more!"

These dimensions are not in the hands of the church's leadership. So, if you fail to have all the measurements of Holy Spirit, this is your fault. You cannot blame your pastor, apostle or your bishop for being small and stuck. This is your responsibility. It's your responsibility to read your Bible and know the riches of your inheritance. This is every person's own salvation—that you must work out. No one can keep you small, but you. You are the master of your own hunger. You are the master of your own thirst. If you fill yourself with the Word of God, discovery takes place. You begin to see the options that are available to you as an heir of God. Stop blaming spiritual leadership for your lack of dimension. Stop blaming the church that you attend for your lack of fullness. This is your responsibility. Holy Spirit led you to this book to enlighten you and give you the assessments needed to see where you are lacking. Width is not all there is. Don't you want more?

Length is also available. This dimension gives you the ability to expand your vision, what you hear, and your ability to know and follow the voice of God. This is paramount to your full development. Length! How long can you pray? How long can you endure? How long can you go through the rough patches of life? Your length can be measured in time. Your length gives you the ability to stay your course. "How long?" is the question most believers ask. You must have length to go to the finish line of your faith. Too many believers are on the sideline of life. They could not endure. They did not have length. They had width, but no length. This dimension of Holy Spirit gives you the advantage over weariness and fainting. Width and length are powerful together. Even though they work well alone, they work best together. Holy Spirit wants you to have width—greatness, bigness, the capacity to do great things. But length gives you advantage over time and timing. How long is the cry of most saints? You promised God! You told me God! But how long must I wait? This dimension of Holy Spirit is a must have if you are to endure the weeks, the years of waiting on your manifestation. It is in the dimension of length that you develop patience, and in patience, you possess your faith. Dreams don't die, but dreamers quit. If you want victory over quitting, if you want victory over complaining and frustration of your season of manifestation, this dimension of length will give you advantage over quitting. and walking away from dreams and visions.

Yes, you have the width. You know what God said. You heard it and it's been verified. But you didn't have length. You aborted many things, started new things without completing other things, because this dimension was lacking in your life. Length is the dimension that gives you the victory over time. And that's not all. The dimension of depth must be pursued.

Depth is what gives your life the quality and intensity. In the marketplace, there is a department in most businesses called quality control. This is where inspection is done to make sure all components are up to the standard of the design and original intent. It takes time to inspect for quality. While you are developing length, there also must be depth so that your life can pass inspection. Quality is better than quantity. In this dimension, you will always feel forced to do better. Reexamine what you're producing. Can it take inspection? Does it have intensity? Is it lacking integrity? It looks good on the surface, but can it withstand storms that will surely come? Quality control is the job of Holy Spirit. Your products, your life, your character, your vision is not the only one. But the uniqueness of what you bring to the earth has been inspected by Holy Spirit and it will not fizzle or fail under pressure. This is depth—the roots of your life. The roots go deep into the soil, where nutrition and hydration occur. You're not flimsy or faltering under the storms of life because your roots are deep. You have the dimension of width. You have the dimension of length. And now, you have the dimension of depth—the invincibility of your faith is because of this dimension of depth. Not for one moment should you think that because you are smart, gifted or talented, that your life will escape the inspection of quality control. When God finally puts you on display, on the shelf for others to see you, the weightiness of who He is in you has been created by repetitive review and examination. You will not go out half done. You may think you're ready. Others may tell you you're ready. But there's no depth. And depth takes time. This is the dimension that really makes the difference in all that you do. Never overlook the dimension of depth and how this dimension of Holy Spirit in your life gives you advantage over the other presentations that may look like you, have your same talent, have your same gift, but have no weight. The glory of God is weighty. The presence of God is weighty. This dimension is weighty. It separates the shallow. It separates weight from depth. Pursue it with your entire mind and all of your strength. What you have is shallow. Shallow doesn't last. This dimension is imperative.

Depth is developed through suffering and persecution. Depth is delivered only to those who have gone through painful seasons, without complaining. Everyone goes through painful seasons. But not everyone goes through without complaining. When you understand that depth dimension is only developed in seasons of agony, abandonment, rejection, you'll stop complaining. And say, "Oh! This is depth. This is what I need."

You'll change your attitude and welcome it. The last thing you want to be is shallow. You'll stop complaining about how people treat you. You'll stop complaining about what people say about you, because you are developing the dimension of depth, and your roots are going deep. And you'll come to a place of satisfaction that whatever you are enduring is going to be worth it. Settle it in your mind and your heart that this dimension is worth everything it will cost you.

So, you want to go high! You want to go up! You have longed for this. This dimension is the most desired. But pause for just a moment and consider that it is the last dimension, not the first, in order of sequence and apprehension. You will never apprehend height without width, length and depth preceding it. But we want to go up. You want to be elevated and promoted. These are the things your heart cries out for. Pick me up! Get me out of this! Why are you preventing me from going to my height? Doesn't this sound immature to you? It's like a baby in a crib, crying with hands lifted up, extended high, "Pick me up!" But it is immature of you to think this will happen first. That's out of sequence. That is out of order. Height is the last dimension that you will obtain. This dimension of height can be very destructive if it is not accompanied by the first three dimensions. Height alone without depth, width and length will cause you to be top heavy. It will cause you to be arrogant and prideful. It will cause you to rest on your own merits, saying, "My talent got me here." Someone will look at you and say, "How brilliant you are! How amazing you are!" and with height alone, it will go to your head. You will become so top heavy that you will fall just from the gravity and weight of your own arrogance. So, Holy Spirit deliberately only gives height to those who have pursued width, length and depth first.

You may ask, "What's the advantage of that?" I'm glad you asked! Let me tell you the multiple stories of leaders, business owners, marriages and relationships that have faltered and failed. Their carcasses lie in the desert waiting for burial, because they sought this dimension first. Holy Spirit had to remove them. Holy Spirit had to keep others from them because their success was toxic. It was not success given by God, but by their own ability and earthly wisdom. By working their hustle, they got to the height of their success. By manipulating relationships, they got to the height of their success. By lying and misstating the truth, they got to the height of their success. So Holy Spirit had to remove them, everything they touched, failed eventually. It didn't fail because it wasn't good, not because they weren't good, not because it lacked value or essence, but because they pursued height alone. Holy Spirit had to remove their voice; their energy and their effort had to be taken away.

In Genesis 11, when the people built a tower, they had the ability to build a tower to the heavens. The height is what they desired. Because they had unity, talent and ability, they were successful—so much so that the Godhead in the heavens said, *"If we don't stop them, they'll come directly up into the heavens."* Their motives were not pure. It would not glorify God. But instead, it would honor their flesh and own abilities. So, what happened? The Bible says, God stopped them in their tracks and He Himself brought destruction to what they were building. If we tell the truth, we desire height because we want someone to celebrate us. We want people to know we are smart and talented, and that we are called of God. So, we go to build a tower. The height is intriguing to us. Surely, if I build it and stand on the platform of my own height, I will finally arrive and get the applause I so desire. Holy Spirit says no, I'm not allowing you height until you have completed the other dimensions. This dimension is only for those, who, when they are elevated, will honor God with everything in them. What an advantage Holy Spirit gives us—sometimes over ourselves. Not every enemy is external. This dimension of height reveals that we ourselves, and our lust, and our pride, can be the worst enemies we will ever confront. So Holy Spirit gives us advantage over this by placing this dimension at the end of our quest and the last to be achieved. This is not the devil. This is not spiritual warfare against us. This is not the work of Satan to prevent us from doing all that's in us. Your pastor isn't stopping you. Your bishop will not ordain you yet. You will not see this dimension revealed, because our advantage knows and is wise to prevent us from coming into this realm immaturely. Some of your prayers can cease right here and come to the place of acceptance that this is Holy Spirit. Your frustration will be healed right now if you understand that this dimension is not elusive or being blocked by superpowers of hell. You are being protected. You are being loved. You are being treated as a daughter or son of the Most High God. Not even Jesus could be lifted, until He mastered obedience by the things He suffered. In the dimension of height, you must be full of age and have your senses exercised to discern both good and evil.

Discernment must operate at this level. This level is not given to the unskillful. This level is given to those who have been perfected in the Word, in their faith and in their character. The dimension of height can be the death of a person who enters in without the other dimensions and without being mature. This is nothing to play with, because once you have obtained height, there is no room for mistakes and failures of character, wrong choices, temper, attitude, un-forgiveness, bitterness or offense. You cannot bring any of that into this dimension. You cannot be at the zenith of your life and ministry and make mistakes that should have been perfected while you were in obscurity. You will damage too many people. You will mislead too many people. You don't hit the rock at the height of your success. You don't have temper tantrums at the height. You cannot walk around without forbearance for all in this dimension. Your character must be purged of these flaws. You will have to have already mastered them. They no longer dictate your actions or reactions. At the height of who God wants you to be, you have been carefully, deliberately and intentionally working on yourself. You have made all of your mistakes by your lack of wisdom. Your lack of discernment in matters of life has already been done. You hold no grudges now. You have no emotional issues with anyone. You can work in love with everyone. Your childhood problems have been resolved. You are not touchy and easily angered. Your temperament has been mastered and your liabilities are under control. This is when height is opened to you.

When you walk in ankle-deep water, as spoken to us in Ezekiel, the rest of the body is seen. When you walk in knee-deep water, the upper part of your body is still seen. Your upper torso is still visible. When you walk deeper, water is now up to your waist. More of you in the water is now in equal proportions. But the next dimension completely immerses you. The overflow dimension immerses you. You are no longer visible. You are submerged in the water of Holy Spirit. Your voice is His voice. Your thoughts are His thoughts. Your identity has merged with His. What do you want people to see: You, or the water? Holy Spirit is the water. He invites us, little by little, step by step to give Him ultimate control. He will not take it from you. He will offer help to you, but you must trust Him enough to walk into the fullness of who He is until the overflow takes place. None of you is available for scrutiny, identity or celebration. Now, Holy Spirit is totally honored, totally worshipped, totally submitted to, and nothing shall ever be too difficult for you again. The Advantage is now operating in your life and in your will at His optimum capacity.

The dimension of constant overflow is activated.

Bilingual

The day of Pentecost was different from salvation. Religion is a weapon of mass destruction. People can preach, sing well and pray well, but they are not filled with Holy Ghost. The only biblical evidence of the indwelling of Holy Ghost is speaking in tongues. Many people fight the tongues. But when we received Christ, we received the indwelling of Holy Spirit. That is not Pentecost. That is salvation. It's important you understand the difference between the two. No man can be saved except Holy Spirit draw him, and no person can belong to God unless they have His spirit dwelling within. Pentecost came to give you a different measure of Holy Spirit. You can't celebrate Pentecost and ignore the tongues. Billions have received the baptism of Holy Spirit with the evidence of speaking in tongues. Why would the requirements, the evidence, be different for you?

Being indwelt with Holy Spirit is not the same experience as the outpouring or baptism with Holy Spirit. What happened at Pentecost separates it from salvation. I used to think speaking in tongues wasn't for everybody. I thought it was a gift not everyone would receive. Once you have Holy Ghost, you don't argue about whether or not everyone should have it. The only people who argue about speaking in tongues are those who do not. Nobody argues about money when they have money. The only people that argue about money are broke. If you had it, you wouldn't argue about it. You only argue about what you don't have. There are very strong arguments in the church about speaking in tongues that defy the baptism of Holy Spirit. Many people believe they will not, or don't have to, speak in tongues, because they either consider it to be a gift or they have not been given proper information.

I spent a significant part of my life searching for Holy Spirit. I hungered for something more, but I tarried for years. By the time I was 11 or 12 years old, I knew there had to be something else; something greater. I knew I received Jesus Christ, but it wasn't enough. I was still broken. I still struggled in school. I still had peer pressure. My emotions and hormones still ran wild. I knew there had to be something else other than Jesus. I was saved and I knew God spoke to me. But there was still something missing. Over time, God sent the right people to answer my question of what I was missing. As a musician, I watched many people get filled with Holy Ghost. I didn't understand it. I couldn't validate it with Scripture at the time. But I knew it was authentic. I encountered many men of God—pastors, preachers, apostles—who could preach, whoop and holler, but didn't believe in Holy Ghost with the evidence of speaking in tongues. I may have been dismayed, but I wasn't going to be deterred. I kept searching. I kept asking. I read the Bible, but I didn't have the spirit of revelation and knowledge, so I couldn't understand what I read.

If you have received Jesus, you are saved. But Holy Spirit seals what you have experienced through the blood of Jesus. He becomes the guarantor of the revelation of salvation that we will receive in fullness at a later date. Holy Spirit draws and seals. Without Holy Spirit, you have no power. You are saved. You will go to Heaven if you die today, but you don't have any power. You can't overcome your circumstances. You don't have any victory. Holy Spirit came to make you His witness. Holy Spirit wants to use you in birthing out the kingdom. The church, through the form of religiosity, has done away with the gifts of the spirit. So, we don't see the casting out of demons and people vomiting at the altar. We don't see people really experience miracles, signs and wonders. We don't see dead people raised from the dead. We have become comfortable with good preaching, singing and a decent prayer. Many preachers are great orators but have no power.

Acts 6:8 says: *And Stephen, full of faith and power, did great wonders and miracles among the people.* **Acts 6:10-11** *And they were not able to resist the wisdom and the spirit by which he spoke. Then they suborned men, which said, we have heard him speak blasphemous words against Moses, and against God.* Pentecost stirred up the religious right. Pentecost annoyed people. It aggravated people. You can have great conversations about God and people won't fall out with you over it. You can even have great conversations about Jesus without offending anyone. But when you talk about Holy Ghost, you open up the door for all types of perspectives and opinions. Many people graduate from seminary, with the belief, there is no dispensation of Holy Ghost. They are taught that speaking in tongues is not for today's church. But if you try to cancel Christmas, people will kill you. Every 12 months, we put Jesus back in a manger. He is the only baby that never grew up. People will literally leave the church if you say you aren't celebrating it this year. We even make Resurrection Sunday a huge deal.

We continuously hang Him high and stretch Him wide. We keep crucifying Him afresh. Yet,

50 days beyond Resurrection Day, there is no mention of Pentecost.

God never left the church in the hands of pastors. He left the church in the hands of the apostles. The apostles then appointed pastors. There has been a covert attack against Pentecost. There is nothing fought against more than Holy Ghost. **Acts 7:51** *Ye stiffnecked and uncircumcised in heart and ears, ye do always resist the Holy Ghost: as your fathers did, so do ye.* Here, Stephen is not talking to the heathen—he's talking to the religious community. He's talking to the leaders of the synagogues. He is speaking to the paradigm that didn't want to change. He's not talking to the drunk or the drug addict. He's talking to those who controlled the religious gates in that time.

Religion has become a weapon of mass destruction. It destroys your mind and makes you think that there is nothing greater than salvation. Stephen emphasized that the people *always* resisted the Holy Spirit. When people don't have the Holy Ghost, they come up with a replica or a similarity of the Holy Ghost. That's why we love titles and priestly garments. But these things are being used to replace the real power of Holy Spirit. It's being used to make you think the people who wear these garments and have these titles are filled with Holy Ghost. They can scream, but they don't have Holy Ghost. They don't cast out devils. They don't lay hands on the sick. You always know when people don't have Holy Ghost because they don't allow other people to receive Holy Ghost from them. They don't have authentic power so they can't lay hands on you to receive authentic power. They do an altar call to accept Jesus, but they never give a call to receive Holy Ghost. You have many people who are saved, and they've been baptized in Jesus's name, but have not been filled with Holy Ghost. After these people have torn themselves up with heroin, with pornography and with multiple attempts of suicide, they slide into a church and get filled with Holy Ghost and suddenly, their yokes of bondage are destroyed. At this point, they wonder why their first pastor never told them about Holy Ghost.

Acts 7:52 says: *Which of the prophets have not your father's persecuted and they have slain them which showed before of the coming of the Just One? Of whom ye have been now the betrayers and murderers.* Not only have they resisted Holy Spirit, but they murder the baptizer of Holy Ghost. This is a strategic plan of the devil—to fight the church from being filled with Holy

Spirit. I searched far and wide for it. I wanted it so bad I stayed up at night longing and searching for it. I didn't know what to pray for. I didn't know exactly what to say or what to ask for. I wasn't familiar with the language. But I knew there was something else. Everywhere I went, people told me there was nothing more. Even when I visited some Pentecostal churches, they couldn't explain it to me—they just told me to cry out to Jesus and He would give me Holy Spirit. While that was true, they couldn't give me anything of substance to back it.

Until there was a prayer meeting in one of the church mothers' basement, I bombarded Heaven and cried out to God pleading for something more. God made a way for me to get what I needed. I wanted it all! What I saw in the basement, I had never seen in a church. I had to go to a basement to experience the gifts of the spirit. There, a prophetess spoke a word from the Lord that if we praised from our desperation, He would baptize right then and there with Holy Ghost. Now, in my church, we knew how to shout. We knew how to throw off our hats and run. But when you grow up in an environment where the people resist Holy Spirit, you don't even know the vocabulary. But the woman next to me started speaking in tongues and at some point, it dropped on me. When they took me out of the basement, they had to pick me up and carry me out. I wanted it so bad and I had waited so long, that I didn't want a drizzle or a sip of it. I wanted to drink and be drunk with Holy Ghost. It was then that I saw my true calling to the ministry. The year was 1974: 40 plus years of being baptized with Holy Ghost at this writing.

The next few days, I couldn't work. I couldn't cook dinner. I couldn't take care of the children. I was filled with Holy Ghost on a Tuesday night. It was Saturday morning before it broke. The tongues are the evidence. When the Holy Spirit baptizes, there is a sound. You receive Jesus and you may cry. But you cannot receive Holy Ghost without a sound. Whenever a baby is born, we listen for the sound to identify that this is a live birth. Nurses and doctors look to hear a sound after aspirating a baby. If there is no sound, we know it's not a normal birth. Some people want to be baptized in Holy Spirit, but it's not normal for them *not* to speak in tongues. The Bible says, there was a sound as a mighty, rushing wind and the whole room was filled with tongues of fire.

Acts 10:44 says: *"While Peter yet spake these words, the Holy Ghost fell upon all them which heard the word."* While Peter preached, Holy Ghost fell upon them, despite the fact that he didn't want to go. I know you are saved. I know you confessed Jesus as Lord and Savior. But this is not the *within* experience. This is the *upon* experience. When Holy Spirit comes upon you, you receive power. If I drink a bottle of water, it helps me—not you. It lubricates my organs and hydrates my body. It keeps my cells from deflating. The water that is in me is only for me. But when I stand in a shower, now the water is not in me—it is upon me. That makes me attractive to other people. I don't take a shower to please myself. It's for the benefit of those around me. I put on perfume so that I smell good to others. While Peter was teaching, Holy Ghost fell *upon all* those that heard the word. **Acts 10:45** says: *And they of the circumcision which believed were astonished, as many as came with Peter, because that on the Gentiles also was poured out the gift of the Holy Ghost.* They were astonished because the gift of Holy Spirit was poured out upon the Gentiles. They knew they had received Holy Spirit because of the tongues. Otherwise, what evidence do you have that you have received Holy Spirit?

Many people go to dead churches. Shouting is not a sign of Holy Ghost. Dancing is not a sign of Holy Ghost. A good choir and a good sermon are not the signs of Holy Ghost. The evidence that Holy Ghost is upon you is speaking in tongues. There are two applications of tongues. One application of tongues is for public interpretation. The other application of tongues is for your personal edification. **1 Corinthians 14:4** says: *He who speaks in a tongue edifies himself, but he who prophesies edifies the church.* I don't need an interpreter then. But if I stand up to prophesy in a corporate worship experience in tongues, then it must be interpreted so the people can understand the prophecy. When I pray in tongues, I do not have to call for an interpretation. That is the language of my spirit man. Every now and then, God uses someone who is baptized by Holy Spirit to stand in a public service and prophesy in tongues. That requires an interpretation. But you need the tongues just to fill yourself up in your most holy faith. When you pray in the spirit, you pray mysteries. You don't pray what's in your mind.

While you will have some wonderful victories, you will also have some mistakes and failures. But you need to be able to ask Holy Spirit to try you in the area of failure again so that you won't fail at it a second time. You want to be able to overcome. The moment you hear His voice, you should not resist or challenge Him. You don't want to argue with Holy Spirit. You have to get to the point where Holy Spirit can count on you to be absolutely compliant in every situation. **John 16:7** says: *Nevertheless I tell you the truth. It is to your advantage that I go away; for if I do not go away, the Helper will not come to you; but if I depart, I will send Him to you.* Since it is *to* your advantage that means Holy Spirit has gone before you. Holy Spirit runs in front of me. Holy Spirit runs ahead of you. Jesus had His season. After the resurrection, His season was finished. So, if He stayed beyond His season, the season of Holy Spirit could not begin. Speaking in tongues is so necessary. When you pray in tongues, you are not praying intellectually. Your spirit is now praying. **John 20:22** says: *And when He had said this, He breathed on them, and said to them, "Receive the Holy Spirit."* That means you have to receive Holy Spirit. You have to receive His influence. You have to receive what He is trying to say to you. The ministry of Holy Spirit is to change the believer into the same image of Jesus Christ.

You don't have to ask Holy Spirit to change you. Once you receive Him, He is automatically going to change you. I didn't have to ask my mother to cook. She already received me as her child and the responsibilities that came along with that. You don't know what you *really* need Holy Spirit to do. Stop trying to control what Holy Spirit works on and when. We want Holy Spirit to do what we want Him to do. You don't know what, when or how He will work on it. You don't even know how it will look when He's finished. If you're truly going to receive Holy Spirit, you have to stop bossing Him around. You are still trying to own and control some part of what He wants to do in your life. You cannot micromanage Holy Spirit. We don't know the mind of God like Holy Spirit knows the mind of God. The areas in which you think you have your greatest challenges may not be the top priority to God.

If I bring something to you, in order for you to receive it, you have to extend your hands in order to receive it. You have to take your hands off yourself and receive Holy Spirit. You have to accept whatever He does, in the timing that He does it. It won't happen in your timing. Holy Spirit is there to lead *you*, not for you to lead *Him*. Just because you *accept* Holy Spirit does not mean you have received Him. You accept what the Bible says. But you receive Holy Spirit. Furthermore, when you receive Holy Spirit, you can't receive Him and then tell Him to go work on someone else. He is the Spirit of Truth, not you. What you say may not be the truth. But Holy Spirit cannot lie. So, you cannot use Holy Spirit to support your opinion. He is not here to support your motives and opinions. He is here to bring you into truth and into the perfect will of God. You can't give Holy Spirit a list and ask Him to go to work. That may not be what Holy Spirit is ordered to do in your life that day. All you can do is ask Him to command your day and lead you according to God's perfect will.

When you detour from what Holy Spirit has told you to do, you will find yourself right where you wanted to be—but without Holy Spirit. Then, you must go back to where you left Holy Spirit and reconnect to Him. We don't have to give Holy Ghost instructions on His assignment. We don't have to offer suggestions. It's important that we not manipulate the power from the gift of speaking in tongues and being filled with Holy Ghost. When Holy Spirit gives us the advantage, it's to glorify Him, not ourselves. **Luke 24:49** says: *"Behold, I send the Promise of My Father upon you; but tarry in the city of Jerusalem until you are endued with power from on high."* If you get the power without first receiving it, you will surely use the power for your own gain. Holy Spirit is not rude or sassy. That is not His intended use.

The word *endued* is very powerful. When you go to a paint store and ask for a color, they have to mix the paint with a base. When you give them the color stick, they take the base and mix many different colors. Then they put it on a machine to mix the colors and many times, we want them to hurry up. But when they take it off the machine, you no longer see color and base. You see the color on the stick you presented to them. Now it is endued. The store then places a sticker with a name on the top to define what that container has been transformed into. It can never again be separated. It will always be that color. It is the same with Holy Spirit. We are endued. Holy Spirit should become so mixed together in such a way that it can never be extracted from us. When God needs to "color" a situation or "decorate" a moment in time, He can pull us in.

Holy Spirit is not concerned about your rough childhood or marriage. That is the base. But He knows what color He will make you—that which you will become. He also knows the exact base it takes to get that color! For certain colors, you need a dark base. Others require a neutral base. You don't put all colors in the same base. Stop celebrating the base. He knows everything that has happened to us. But He needs that base to get the right tone. When he puts us in a situation, it can't look like someone else's color, because we didn't start with the same base. God is working on decorating the earth with His glory. Each one of us has a distinct contribution to that glory. But we don't have the same contribution. We're not derived from the same base. The glory is defined by how you operate with the base. With all of the disadvantages and the things that should have crippled you, He's still going to use you, and we definitely don't need to give Him instruction.

God doesn't want every room to be crème. He wants red, black and even some green rooms. God does not like all neutral. If that were the case, we'd all have the same testimony. That testimony is unique to your color. Don't be ashamed of it or cover it up. He will use that pain and experience to make a beautiful color. Don't compare your testimony, or your color, to anyone else's. Everyone has a different base! Many times, we are intimidated by the way Holy Spirit uses someone else. We may even try to mimic or imitate them, but you don't know their base. Be your authentic self! Be the authentic you!

When Holy Spirit endues you, there is a sound that is unique to Holy Spirit.

Acts 1:8 says: *And He said to them, "It is not for you to know times or seasons which the Father has put in His own authority. But you shall receive power when the Holy Spirit has come upon you; and you shall be witnesses to Me in Jerusalem, and in all Judea and Samaria, and to the end of the earth."* Many of us want the power, but we don't want the tongues. Peter went into the Upper Room one way and came out as an apostle. He didn't do well under pressure and he suffered from extreme anxiety. But once He was filled in the Upper Room, it changed his whole contents and made Him usable.

Weeping and complaining is not prayer. God wants people to come into His presence and speak His language. His language is not the language of your natural tongue. There is a language of the Spirit that is birthed in you when you are filled with Holy Ghost. When you speak in tongues, your whole life will change. You'll find yourself getting stronger. You'll find that you are able to pray more specifically. You can tell the difference between someone who can only pray in

English and someone who prays in tongues. The one who prays in English has a very emotional, distraught type of prayer. They have great emotional release. But your soul is not your spirit. So even though you've prayed for the issues of your soul, you never tapped into your spirit. You must mature beyond praying your emotions. You have to be baptized with Holy Spirit in order to pray in tongues. Being filled with Holy Spirit is just like driving your car on the road. If I fill up in Michigan and drive to Ohio, when I get back to Michigan, I'll need to fill up the car again. You can't drive on that same tank of gas all week. You would be on the side of the road and someone would have to come and get you. But if I go to the gas station on a regular basis, I'm guaranteed not to run out of gas!

The church has run out of gas. We shouted ourselves right into empty. We danced our way right into empty. We have hollered ourselves right into empty. You have to refill! Don't try to perpetrate and act like you have it if you don't. Don't wrestle with whether or not you have to have it. You need all of what God has to offer you. I couldn't stop smoking. I couldn't stop cursing. I had Jesus and I loved him more than anything. But I didn't have any power. When I got baptized in Holy Ghost, He gave me power—He gave me The Advantage! I was able to subdue the works of my flesh. The baptism of Holy Spirit is the most amazing thing that has ever happened to me in my life. Holy Spirit is my best friend. Jesus may be your best friend. But that is a second-day friend. When people sing about Jesus, records sell. But if they were to sing about Holy Ghost, the records may not sell as easily. So, we pimp Jesus so we can get a Stellar Award or a Grammy. The church is overly religious, and they resist Holy Ghost. They sing the songs of Zion and still take their clothes off at the hotel. They run around the church and curse somebody out in the parking lot. They'll sing the popular gospel songs that come on the radio and still shoot dope in the arm. People know that if they ever get Holy Ghost, it will stop them from their madness. Jesus never promised to deliver you—He only promised to save you. He went back to Heaven once His assignment was complete. All you are is saved.

But when you are filled with Holy Ghost, He will guide you and lead you. He is the Spirit of Truth. Jesus did all He could do. He saved you and reconciled you back to God, but He can't deliver you. It is time out for faking and pretending. Get filled with the real thing. Get filled with Holy Ghost!

Then, and only then, will you have power!

Waiting to Exhale

In 1995, the romantic drama, *Waiting to Exhale* was released. Directed by Forest Whitaker, this film had an all-star cast, including Whitney Houston, Angela Bassett, Loretta Devine and Lela Rochon. All of the women were at various stages of both life and love. But periodically, each woman would exhale in a certain part of the movie—most times, when being intimate with a man. Likewise, when we are endued with Holy Spirit, we should be able to exhale. We should be able to let our guards down. We should be able to fully trust in whatever direction in which He leads us. When we exhale, we breathe out and release energy. The women in *Waiting to Exhale* all basically "held their breath" until the day they were comfortable in a committed relationship with a man—or so they thought. However, it's vital to note that every time they exhaled, whether they stayed with the men in their lives or not, the relationship between the four women grew stronger over time.

When a baby is born, it is vitally important that the baby cries within thirty seconds to a minute after it has been birthed. When the baby is inside the mother's uterus, the baby does not breathe through its own lungs—it breathes through the umbilical cord. Even if a baby does not cry immediately after birth, the nurse then suctions the nose and lungs of amniotic fluid and secretions so the baby can cry clearly. Not only does the baby cry because he or she is probably hungry, but the baby has now transitioned from a dark, cozy environment to an unfamiliar place full of light. If the baby doesn't cry, doctors immediately know that something is wrong with the baby. The baby may not have strong lungs. There may be a physical ailment. The baby may not cry due to stress and depression from a traumatic pregnancy. Sometimes, the baby may not even cry because of the medications the mother has been sedated with during the delivery process. But a baby born that is born healthy will surely cry and exhale.

Genesis 2:7 says: *And the Lord God formed man of the dust of the ground, and breathed into his nostrils the breath of life; and man became a living soul*. When God created the heavens and the earth, He said, "Let there be." When it was time to create the birds of the air and the fish of the seas, He said, "Let there be." Even when He created every other living thing, He called to the earth to bring forth every living creature of its kind. He did not have to breathe life into the heavens and the earth. He did not have to breathe life into the fish of the sea or the birds of the air. He simply spoke, and then it *was*. Immediately after He spoke something into existence, it was there. But even after He formed Adam, he still took the time to breathe life into him. It was not until He breathed into him that the Bible says, Adam became a living being. The animals are living. The birds and the fish are all living. But there was something special about man that caused God to breathe life into us.

Man was given charge over all of the earth—including the beasts of the field, birds of the air, fish of the seas and even every creeping thing. That means man even has charge over the caterpillar and the worm that crawls on the ground. Man was formed of the dust and God breathed into the nostrils of man. Likewise, when a baby is born, the nostrils sometimes have to be cleared of mucus in order for the baby to successfully exhale. Human beings naturally breathe in and out through the nose. We don't have to breathe through our mouths. Unless there is something medically wrong, we can breathe in and out through our noses. However, if you ever get a cold or struggle with asthma, you sometimes gasp for air through your mouth. When you need to exhale an excessive amount of air, you do so through the mouth. If you run a marathon or participate in any form of sport, the coach will train you to breathe in through your nose and exhale out through your mouth. I'd imagine that when God breathed into man, Adam exhaled out through his mouth.

It's also important to note that man was *formed*; he was not spoken into existence. God spoke light into existence and divided it from darkness. He spoke dry land and the rivers into existence. But he took the time to *form* man—in His own image—from the dust of the ground. At a funeral, when the remains of a human body are laid to rest, the funeral directors usually commit the body back to the earth by saying, "Earth to earth, ashes to ashes, dust to dust."

As a person nears death, their breathing may become substantially heavier. They may even be to the point of panting like a dog as life leaves the body. This means the organs are slowly shutting down. When a person dies, they die with their mouth open. They have taken their final breath—their final exhale—in the natural realm. The jaw becomes relaxed and the mouth opens. It is during funeral preparation that the mouth and eyes are closed shut.

In ancient Greek, the word *pneuma* means breath. In the religious context, it means spirit or soul, the term *ruach*, often referenced in the Old Testament, means breath, wind or spirit. God formed everything in the earth, as well as man, within six days. On the seventh day, He rested. But the Bible doesn't mention God breathing breath into man until **Chapter 2 of Genesis**. Man already existed, but after God breathed the breath of life into him, now he was both a natural and spiritual being. Had God not breathed into man, he would have been alive, but his soul would not be alive. He would not have access to eternal life. After a man dies and has been put into the ground, his spirit still lives. It is simply at rest until the Lord descends from Heaven for the second coming. In **1 Thessalonians 4:15-17**, *For this we say unto you by the word of the Lord, that we which are alive and remain unto the coming of the Lord shall not prevent them which are asleep. For the Lord himself shall descend from heaven with a shout, with the voice of the archangel, and with the trump of God: and the dead in Christ shall rise first: Then we which are alive* *and remain shall be caught up together with them in the clouds, to meet the Lord in the air: and so shall we ever be with the Lord.*

The Lord doesn't make this promise to the birds of the air or the fish of the sea. He doesn't make the same promises to the beasts of the field or the creeping, crawling things. The promise only applies to man. When we are born, we exhale. When we die, we exhale. But it is Holy Spirit that will help you master what you were set on the earth to do. We were all predestined with a distinct purpose and calling. Although some of us may seem to hold the same types of gifts, a different level of grace is given to each individual. There are many great singers, dancers and preachers. There are various levels of doctors and lawyers, even though, they all hold the same title. There is something within you that only you can do, *in the way that you do it*. The Lord is very strategic about His plans for our lives and what He wants to do through us. But we can't do all God has called us to do without Holy Ghost leading and guiding us daily.

Since the Lord breathed life into man, that which we do in the earth is another form of exhaling. Children, and even some young adults, have to be led by the guidance of their parents. They may not be sure of their God-given purpose and destiny. But over time, as they mature into whom God has called them to be, they exhale their gifts into the earth. When a baby's nose is stopped up, the parent may blow into their mouth to clear the nose passages. Likewise, if you suck in through your nose, anything that is there now rests at the back of the mouth.

When God breathed into man, He breathed into him knowledge. He breathed into him grace and favor. Without that one breath, life as we know it would not exist. When you realize your true calling and the true purpose that God placed you in the earth to fulfill, you will run full speed ahead with it, without a doubt. You'll walk more confidently. You'll talk more confidently. More importantly, you'll be more sensitive to the direction of Holy Spirit. You won't go where He tells you not to go. You won't associate with people whom He tells you to leave alone. You'll be more careful of the company you keep. You'll be more conscious of the words you speak.

Proverbs 18:21 says: *Death and life are in the power of the tongue: and they that love it shall eat the fruit thereof.* The words you exhale either give life, or they kill. This doesn't necessarily happen overnight though. If a person says they are broke every day, if they never confess that they have enough to meet their needs or more than enough, they will always be broke. What they constantly release, or exhale, into the atmosphere, is that which will be. Likewise, if a person constantly confesses that they are the head and not the tail, that they are victorious in every situation, and that they have more than enough, that is the direction their life will follow. This is why the Word of God reminds us to keep our minds stayed on the things that are pure, things that are lovely, things that are of good report. If you focus on positive things, positive words of affirmation are prone to come out of your mouth. But if you take in negative energy, get emotionally caught up in the bad reports on the nightly news, and hang around negative people, your words will reflect just that. Watch your mouth! God breathed life into man, but what we exhale has the potential to kill if we're not careful.

What will you breathe out into the earth in between the very first time you inhale and the moment you exhale for the very last time? Our days are numbered from conception to death. Everyone is not given the same measure of life. Not everyone is given the same measure of the same gift. There are some singers who can hit higher notes than others and it sounds melodious. If another artist tries it, and they aren't equipped with the same amount of grace in the gift, it won't sound so well. It is up to you, through Holy Spirit, to master the gifts that He placed on the inside of you.

The Finishing Anointing

In **John 17:4,** Jesus speaks: *"I have brought you glory on earth by finishing the work you gave me to do."* In **John 19:30**, Jesus said, *"It is finished."* The perfecting of our lives is something we all should look forward to. By perfecting, I don't mean a life without mistakes. I don't mean that you have reached a point in life where you have lost your humanity, and no longer are subject to flaws. By perfecting, I mean every day you are closer and closer to completing the assignment of your life.

1 Corinthians 12:4-11 speaks to the gifts of Holy Spirit. The tools for finishing are very simply seen through the gifts of Holy Spirit. I want to show you how to utilize the finishing tools to get you to a place of complete satisfaction in the Lord. There are nine gifts of Holy Spirit that are deposited within every believer upon receiving the baptism of Holy Spirit. The baptism of Holy Spirit is seen in **Acts Chapter 2** where Holy Spirit came upon each of them, filled them, engulfed them, endued them; and they began to speak with other tongues as Holy Spirit gave them the ability. This is the beginning of the finishing anointing in your life. When a person receives Jesus Christ as their savior, it is to remove the penalty, consequences and judgment of sin from their lives. But you still don't have tools for finishing. This comes with receiving the Gift of Holy Spirit. He is our gift. Not just the indwelling of Holy

Spirit that comes to every person to live inside of them, who confesses Jesus Christ as their Savior by faith. I'm speaking of the outpouring component. The baptism component that comes to give power to live the life God originally ordained.

With baptism, there are nine manifestations or gifts of Holy Spirit.

These are your finishing tools:

Knowing Gifts

❖ **Word of Knowledge:** The ability given to you to know what you would never know. It usually deals with a glimpse of the past and the present and gives insight.

❖ **Word of Wisdom:** The ability given to glimpse the future and how the events of the past will work out for the purposes of God.

❖ **Discernment:** The ability to know the root causes and spirit life behind every event, emotion or occurrence of life. This manifestation of Holy Spirit is the true sign of maturity.

Speaking Gifts

❖ **Prophecy:** The ability to edify and speak comfort and encouragement by Holy Spirit's leading, without previous knowledge. You will speak to a person or situation and bring the mind of God.

❖ **Tongues:** The ability to speak a language or dialect for the purpose of prayer, prophecy and worship that cannot be interfered with by satanic forces. This gift edifies the spirit of the believer and deposits in that spirit the mind and will of God.

❖ **Interpretation:** When tongues are used in a corporate setting, and sometimes in personal prayer, interpretation will come by Holy Spirit to unfold what was said in tongues. This is particularly useful in a corporate setting where prophecy, word of knowledge or word of wisdom, is being used to perfect that body of people.

Power

❖ **Faith:** This is not a common salvation faith that all believers have. This is supernaturally charged faith to do exploits. In a time of reservation or skepticism, this gift will kick in and manifest the power of God.

❖ **Healing:** The manifestation of healing for the body, mind and spirit. Physical healings, emotional healings, are all the fruit of this gift in operation.

❖ **Working of Miracles:** This is the power gift seen in the book of Acts, where exploits were done by the laying on of hands, casting out of demons, raising the dead and all manners of demonstrations of the power of God. Miracles working in our lives are evidence of God's love to intervene against human error.

These are our finishing tools. These should be operational in our lives, as the spirit wills. As a believer moves toward maturity, these gifts are activated more and more in our daily lives. These gifts are not just for church services and revivals. It's not just for mission trips and crusades. They should be fully engaged in our daily lives. When you see the operation of these gifts in your day to day life, the rough edges will smooth out. You will stop making mistakes because you will discern early what to avoid. Holy Spirit will use words of knowledge and words of wisdom in your business dealings. As you negotiate contracts, mortgages and opportunities, prophecy is needed and will come into play.

These finishing tools are used much like in construction. The roughing done by subcontractors is at the beginning stage of building a new home. Everything is wide open. Lines are running everywhere. You see people digging holes and you see the beams going into the ground. It doesn't yet look like a dwelling place. This is the beginning of the building process. But after the walls go up and all of the holes and openings have now been closed, it is time for the general contractor to call for the finishers. Those are the people who come in and see the improprieties and see where it can be corrected and smoothed out to beautify the dwelling place. These are the painters, the molders, and the people who lay the carpet. They dress the home. They stage it for the new residents to occupy. This is the beautification process. The dwelling place finally is ready to be occupied. It's ready to fulfill its original purpose.

The tools of Holy Spirit given to you and I will beautify us with His salvation. Many of us are still in the rough stages. Our holes are still showing. Wires are still hanging. We're saved, but we are not fully yet occupied by Holy Spirit. We cannot fulfill our purpose in life until the finisher comes and brings His tools. These gifts of Holy Spirit have saved my life on so many occasions. They have guided me and opened my eyes to see things I would have otherwise missed. I've been able to move in power and faith at supernatural levels. But it's the finishing anointing. Without the finishing anointing upon your life, you will never get to the point of purpose and satisfaction.

Why were you born? What problem were you born to solve? As you have grown in the knowledge of Christ, and have discovered your divine destiny, you should seek for the day when you reach your satisfaction point. When you stand and look at your life and say, "God, I've done the work. I've put in the time. I left a mark in my generation that can't be erased." Now, I want to live in the bounty of knowing that I pleased God. I'm no longer caught up in foolishness or distracted by things that keep me off target. I am focused. I am committed. I have done the hard work and the grunt labor of birthing my divine purpose. With the advantage in my life, I have navigated through life's waters—around alligators, vultures, whales and crocodiles. By faith, I have mastered my human spirit. I have disciplined myself to recognize my liabilities and the landmines that would take me out. I'm on the other side of repentance now. My prayer life is not consumed with things I did wrong. I'm on the other side of that now. I'm living out God's best for my life. I'm still young enough to enjoy the fruit of my labor. I'm satisfied.

Holy Spirit has given me the mysteries and divine plans, and daily I have walked them out. I have gone places I didn't know I would go. I have accomplished things I never thought I could.

I'm in coaching mode. I'm raising protégés. I am raising women of strength, purpose and destiny. This is the finishing anointing job in our lives. He is the perfecter of our purpose and God's best for us.

Several years ago, vision boards became very popular. I'll tell you a secret—just between you and me. I never thought that was the way to reach my goals. As I go to magazines and cut the pictures of the things that I want in my life—the houses, the cars, the clothing, the popularity - and put it all on the vision board, at what point do I accept Holy Spirit's role in my life to tell me and guide me into what God wants for me? So, the vision board experience is just futile and recreation. Who I really need to consult with is Holy Spirit. How many people are in the valley of discouragement right now because they cannot make sense of their day-to-day purpose? They chase after pipe dreams and do things God never intended for them to do.

I'm not saying ambition is bad or wrong. But ambition without the advantage is utter failure. Many people suffer from mental illness, depression and mental breakdown because they're chasing things they want. They've never desired to do the things God put them in the earth to do. When Jesus came into the earth, He didn't have to wonder what He was here to do. His assignment was clear. With the help of Holy Spirit, Jesus was able to finish what God sent Him to do. There is great peace in knowing why you're here and why you're alive—not millions of other tasks and diversions that leave you unfulfilled. Jesus knew that He had come to save God's people from their sins. Healing was not the agenda. Casting out devils was not the agenda. Raising the dead was not the agenda. He did those things to fulfill what the prophets had spoken of Him. He did this to prove that He was indeed Christ, The Messiah. He didn't get distracted and become a world-renowned healer. He knew He was on the earth for a purpose. He knew what problem He was born to solve. He did that and only that.

The testimony of the Scriptures tells us He was well pleasing to His Father. How did Jesus get to the point of saying, "It is finished"? He got there by the help of Holy Spirit. His entire life was governed by Holy Spirit. When Holy Spirit came upon Mary, she conceived without a man. He was guided by His entire life by Holy Spirit. We saw Jesus praying long hours alone without disciples present, because He sought direction from His Father. His primary goal was to please the Father. He knew this would mean He would complete His assignment.

We want to please God—doing our own thing. We want God to be pleased with all our ideas and suggestions. But

God's help is available to use when we get on purpose and get in line with His plan for our lives. Holy Spirit is most profitable to us in the Will of God. Everything Holy Spirit will do when we are out of His will is to bring us back into the center of God's will. That's where our success lies. That's where our faith works at optimum level. That is where we see the greatest success—in the will of God. Holy Spirit has spoken to me many times, saying, "Is that what God said? Is this what you should be working on?" Sometimes, I'm startled. At that very moment, I am convinced I am doing something great and profitable for God. Then Holy Spirit will whisper this question that stops me in my tracks.

Sometimes I laugh because I know He is asking me a rhetorical question. What He's really doing is redirecting my energy and resources. He knows the mind of God. He is the Spirit of Truth. And He has been given to know all things that Jesus knows and reveal those things to me. The moment I digress from my assignment, the advantage quickly brings my attention back to focus by questions, gentle nudging and prods. What a wonderful gift to have the voice of God at all times in my ear! How many mistakes have I avoided? How many millions of dollars have I saved by simply listening and obeying Holy Spirit? When we hear His voice in our ear, we must develop a quick response as a normal reflex to cooperate immediately. We can't fight, grieve, or quench the voice of Holy Spirit.

I had to learn this over the years because I'd struggle in my mind. My soul wrestled and justified what I wanted to do. But I've learned how to abound and abase. I've learned to submit on contact when He speaks. This saves me time, money, relationships and more. At the end of the day, the Spirit of Truth Himself was navigating around the potholes of life. When I cooperate with Holy Spirit, it always works out great!

On the cross, as Jesus was dying, He breathed His last breath and indicated after much agony: "It is finished." I don't want to leave this earth and not have the same last three words.

I don't believe Jesus meant my life is finished. I don't believe He was speaking of death. He was speaking of the assignment. "I did it! It's accomplished! No one will have to come after me and do what I left undone! It is finished. The debt is paid! God and man reconciled again. The same glory that was mine in the beginning, before I came into this earth, will now be mine again." With a short life of 33 and a half years, with only three years of active ministry, He didn't endure unnecessary struggles and foolishness. He got it done. Jesus needed Holy Spirit to get Him to the cross. Jesus needed Holy Spirit to raise Him from the dead. Jesus needed Holy Spirit to keep Him from the distractions of human life. Jesus needed Holy Spirit to keep Him engaged to the Father's Will for His life. Jesus needed Holy Spirit to perform the miracles and the supernatural works that would convince the unbelievers. Jesus didn't fight. He didn't argue. He didn't struggle with the haters. He relied upon Holy Spirit to guide Him, protect Him, and to be to Him the GPS that would get him back to the Father with the completed price of redemption.

Now if Jesus relied upon Holy Spirit, you and I must tap into the secret. Herein lies real success. The ability to have Holy Spirit as our advantage is the key to Zoe life, which is the life of God. That life is a good life. It's a sweet life. It's not without struggles. But it's always victorious. With Holy Spirit guiding, He will always produce a Godly outcome. Most of us want a life without pain. A life without battles. A life without trauma, tears. We certainly do not want a life where we have to wait and ponder and engage our faith and be still and know that God is God. This delusional expectation that once we get saved, and give our lives to Jesus Christ, we shouldn't have to hurt. We shouldn't have to go through anything. I want to be wealthy without work. I want to be pain free, devil free and struggle free. Are you serious? Do you really think you've been given the power of Holy Spirit to live an easy life?

The powerful, creative Holy Spirit is there to help us in these situations, not to prevent them. He is to develop the character and nature of Christ; to perfect us while we're having this human experience. We learn not to rely upon our comfort as a gauge. We actually rely upon Holy Spirit to guide us and to be our gauge. Whatever comes our way, we learn to hear His voice in everything and every moment. I listen to Him so intensely that even when I'm in trouble and trauma, I know it's working for my good because the finishing anointing is still with me and has not left. If you don't know why you were born, there is only one person on earth who can tell you. If you don't know what problem you have been born to solve, there is only one person in the universe who knows the answer. Our parents can't tell us. Preachers can't tell us. The prophets can't tell us, and our friends can't tell us. Only the Spirit of Truth knows all truth that pertains to you.

I firmly believe that I have lived my purpose. Holy Spirit whispered to me many years ago what problem I was born to solve. He said to me, "Preach the gospel. Heal the sick. Cast out devils. And deliver my people from religious bondage." This was in 1977 in an out-of-body death experience. I was diagnosed with cervical cancer and was rushed to the hospital, hemorrhaging to death. I had two small children to raise. I was terrified I would leave them in the hands of my parents to raise because I was going to die. I remember as I turned my face to the wall and walked out of my body into a dark tunnel, I was terrified. It was cold. I didn't know where I was. Suddenly, a bright light appeared that was so white that I couldn't even identify its intensity. It was warming to my cold body. I walked toward this light.

I heard a voice say, "Stop! Where are you going?" I said, "I'm coming home!" A hand came out as if to literally stop me from proceeding any further. I saw a hole in the middle of the hand. The voice said, "Go back. We are not ready for you here. I have called you to be an apostle to my people. Preach the gospel! Heal the sick. Cast out devils. Deliver my people from religious bondage."

I remember bowing to my knees. Under this bright light were two feet with big holes. I walked backwards, the way I had come until I was no longer in the tunnel, not knowing that for those moments, I had literally died.

Back on the side of human life, they were resuscitating me. I didn't know then that it had been three days. I'd received several blood transfusions. I awakened with tears on my face saying, "Yes, Lord!" I had been running from God. I didn't want to preach. I was happy with my life as a professional registered nurse. I had a very profitable career. I had aspirations of being a top nurse in the navy. I wanted to wear the uniform. I wanted to help people in the field. All of my life, as a little girl I wanted to be a nurse. I was intrigued with the uniform. I loved it. I knew I would spend my life in nursing. But that inevitable moment in that tunnel changed my life. I knew that if I was going to have peace, I had to get with God's plan for my life.

Sometimes God will go out of His way to arrest us to be what He always wanted us to be. I'm grateful today for that moment in time. It was a long journey back to health with several surgeries and treatments. I was disabled from work. I was unable to raise my children. But I can honestly say, now, that saved my life. I could have been a lot of things. I have a lot of talent and I'm pretty smart. But none of those things would be pleasing to God. They would be good things, but it wasn't the purpose for which I was born.

I wonder as you read this, are you thinking about finishing the work God gave you to do? Are you emulating somebody else? Are you trying to be fulfilled by living vicariously through others? Are you enamored by the life someone else is living so much so that you are trying to duplicate that? You can never finish what God never started. You can never hear the words *well done, good and faithful servant* if you don't get to the point of doing what you were born to do. The only person in the universe who can help you with this is Holy Spirit. Not only will He reveal to you what it is, but He will give you power, stamina and endurance to finish it. He is the finishing anointing, and He will work with you to complete the task God has ordained for you to do. There is so much peace, so much joy and satisfaction in being able to finish and end your days here on earth, knowing that you are pleasing and have left a mark on your generation that cannot be erased. Get to know Holy Spirit. Make that your goal in life. When you have finished reading these pages, make sure this is not just another book on your shelf. Ask Holy Spirit to tell you why you were born. Where should I live? Where should I go? What should I pursue? Ask Him to show you, and He will do it.

Luke 11:9-13 is one of my favorite passages of Scripture, *"So I say to you: Ask and it will be given to you; seek and you will find; knock and the door will be opened to you. For everyone who asks receives; the one who seeks finds; and to the one who knocks, the door will be opened. "Which of you fathers, if your son asks* *for[a] a fish, will give him a snake instead? Or if he asks for an egg, will give him a scorpion? If you then, though you are evil, know how to give good gifts to your children, how much more will your Father in heaven give the Holy Spirit to those who ask him?"*

Stop. Ask right now for the Gift of the Holy Ghost.

Epilogue

We are living in exciting times. Times that we have never seen before—for the church and the believer. These are the days where revival in every aspect is coming like floods. Spiritual conversions, financial wealth transfers, believers being promoted to opportunities that before were shut off in media, arts and entertainment. These times were prophesied in scriptures in **Joel Chapter 2-** *"in the last days I will pour out my Spirit."* We must understand our relationship with Holy Spirit is paramount in order to be connected, and be a part of what God is doing. Nobody will be used in these last days by God that is only saved by the blood of Jesus. You will have to enter into relationship with Holy Spirit to be an active participant in this Third Day outpouring of Holy Spirit on planet earth.

In order for me to explain my excitement, you need to understand the Third Day outpouring. The first day is defined as the time of Old Testament rules, regulations and encounters with Jehovah God. These were difficult days. There was no complete freedom between God and man. It gave birth to the Second Day and Jesus Christ's earthly ministry of 33 years. God the Father corrects His relationship with man by the sacrifice of His son, Jesus.

Jesus came in the flesh to show man the love of God and the redeeming power of love. The first day was dark and without hope. There was no access. There was no joy.

Man was so separated from God that God dealt through judgment, death, doom and destruction. But on the Second Day, Jesus comes to change the image and redefine the brand previously given of God. God was horrible and to be feared. Jesus comes to rebrand the Godhead in such a way that it made Him unbelievable as God. But the Second Day was the necessary bridge to bridge man and God's relationship.

But all of this leads us to the Third Day. It began on the Day of Pentecost. Pentecost changed everything. It changed the world, the economy, the allocation of power and influence. Pentecost was a game-changer, a defining moment that now, you and I as believers, can live in the benefits and fruitfulness of the Third Day. The Third Day church is the most powerful church that has ever existed. Every man and woman are now equal. All prejudice is done away with. There is no bond or free, male or female. It was done away with at Pentecost. By the Spirit, we are all Abraham's children. Although doctrine and religion are still in place in some context, those strongholds are coming down because of Pentecost. You can see it everywhere. You see it in nations. You see it in the infrastructure of the church. You see it as you watch the motions of revival take over the land. So, you want to be engaged. You don't want to miss this by rejecting Holy Spirit. Becoming knowledgeable of all He provides to you as a believer and the greater life He offers after salvation.

I am amazed as I traveled at how many Jesus-loving people don't understand they need a relationship with

Holy Spirit. For the most part, they are clueless. They've never been taught on gifts of the Spirit. They've never seen the signs and miracles. We've limited ourselves to good teaching and preaching, without manifestation of Holy Spirit. Third Day revival marks the world. You need to be connected and study Holy Spirit throughout Scripture. You need to read books on Holy Spirit, and I will give a bibliography for references that will grow you up. Attend a Bible-believing, Holy Ghost manifestation church where you see miracles weekly, where you experience prophecy and tongues with interpretation of tongues. Special messages given to the church by God through human beings who are endued with Holy Spirit given to encourage, edify and comfort the parish. Why live on the Third Day and only tap into the benefits of day 2? Why not get all that God desires you to have? Jesus, your Savior, and Holy Spirit, your Advantage. Make this your pursuit. Wake up every morning and say out of your mouth, "Good morning, Holy Spirit! I engage you today to guide me into all truth." Give Him the right to fully participate in all your decisions and daily affairs. This is life-changing.

I read the book by Benny Hinn, "Good Morning, Holy Spirit," and his journey to know Holy Spirit for himself. That book changed my life. I began to run for every resource that I could find on Holy Spirit. As God would have it, I read every book by Katherine Kuhlman. I read Amy Semple McPherson's story and the miracles that God used her to manifest during her ministry. It took me over to other works that were on Holy Spirit, including:

- ❖ R. A. Torrey's "The Presence & Work of Holy Spirit"
- ❖ Don Basham's "A Handbook on Holy Spirit Baptism"
- ❖ R. T. Kendall's "Holy Fire"
- ❖ Bishop Fred Addo's "40 Names of the Holy Spirit"
- ❖ Oral Roberts' "Holy Spirit in the Now"
- ❖ Kenneth Hagin's "Understanding the Holy Spirit"
- ❖ R.W. Schambach's "Miracle"
- ❖ Kenneth Wilson's "The Baptism of the Holy Spirit as a Clinical Intervention
- ❖ Randy Clark's "The Essential Guide to the Power of the Holy Spirit"

I've read hundreds more, and continue to read, because I am yet learning about the life of Holy Spirit. So, I want to challenge you to never give up. Never stop searching and digging and learning about Holy Spirit and His advantage in your life. Keep learning. Keep digging. Keep searching. Keep reading.

Remember Your Advantage is *not just for church or religious life,* but He is your wisdom and guide in all areas of life; relationships, finances, career decisions, parenting, choosing a spouse, choosing a school, real estate, business, dreams and visions, buying a car, investments, health and wellness, in other words EVERYTHING. Holy Spirit is God. He knows everything about everything. He is the wisest person in the universe. He is the Spirit of Truth and He knows ALL things. Consult Him for everything. He is your Advantage or everything disqualifying factor and liability that can block you or make you look ill-equipped or unprepared. Holy Spirit gives us the advantage over every situation, so that we are never at the mercy of anything. Make Him your most intimate, personal trusted confidante and friend. Ask Him any question. Speak to Him daily and inquire of His understanding. Stop making decisions without His counsel. Learn to speak to Him and listen to Him about all areas of your life. He is your Gift and your Advantage; the promise of the Father to assure your victory and smooth success while you are earth bound.

In closing, this is my prayer for you. **Ephesians 1:18-20**: *The eyes of your understanding being enlightened; that ye may know what is the hope of his calling, and what the riches of the glory of his inheritance in the saints, And what is the exceeding greatness of his power to us-ward who believe, according to the working of his mighty power, Which he wrought in Christ, when he raised him from the dead, and set him at his own right hand in the heavenly places.* This power is Holy Spirit's power and I want Him to pulse through your life from this day forward. That your eyes would be open, and your heart would be tender to work with Holy Spirit for the rest of your life. Don't argue with Him or fight Him. Engage Him, love Him and commune with Him until Christ is formed in you and you fulfill your God-given purpose. Speak in tongues every day, at least one hour every day. Rev up your spiritual life by speaking in tongues daily. Greet Him as, "Good Morning, Holy Spirit!" If you have not received the gift with speaking in tongues, ask Him for both the Baptism and the experience. If you ask you shall receive Him.

Most of all, my prayer is that you live knowing The Advantage for yourself in a personal way, that you see His expressions and nuances in all the ways He speaks to you. That you respect Him and follow His lead then share Him with everyone you know until the whole earth is filled with the Glory of the Lord as the waters cover the sea and the next wave and outpouring of Pentecost engulfs every living person before the imminent return of Jesus Christ.

Now, go create your own adventure *"Living With The Advantage."*